THE CAPE SCOTT STORY

The Cape Scott Story

by Lester R. Peterson

MITCHELL PRESS / VANCOUVER

Contents

Foreword

Some readers may well consider this book a study in *minutia* and to a degree this is so. For British Columbia is a large province and to chronicle the story of the northern tip of Vancouver Island is certainly a specialized undertaking. But a wide set of forces and motivations have been at play for nearly two centuries and there are specific locales in which a detailed examination of "local" history reveals the changing forces which have been at work over a long span of time in this province.

The Cape Scott Story is such a study and it is fortunate that its author, by virtue of a family association with the area from the early days of settlement, has completed the task for which he was so particularly qualified. He has done us a real service and thereby broadened our understanding of the history of British Columbia.

Of recent years there has been a growing interest in the history and contributions of the varied ethnic groups that have contributed so significantly to the development of our province. Again Mr. Peterson has made a real contribution. The full story of the Danish settlement at Cape Scott has long needed to be told. The high courage of the men and women who ventured into the wilderness at the turn of the century is not to be minimized, ill-starred and tragic as its ultimate consequence may have been.

This is more than a chronicle of that undertaking. The full panorama — from the impact upon our Indian peoples of the coming of explorers and fur traders to World War II R.C.A.F. activity in the area and more recently concern with protection of our ecological heritage — has come under the view of the author. So it is with appreciation that I commend this book to the reader.

WILLARD E. IRELAND
Provincial Librarian and Archivist

CHAPTER I

Cape Scott is a finger, probing out into the Pacific Ocean beyond the closed fist of Vancouver Island. It beckons those who near it from the sea to touch its shores, and points the way to sea again for all who choose to land. Stretching both north and west, it is a crossroads. What it saw in ages past we can only guess at, and can only imagine the voyagers who came, and paused, and went again, leaving no trace. Those who came later are also gone; but they have left their marks, and of them we know.

During the past four hundred million years or so, a great part of the continent of North America has played a sort of hide-and-seek game with its surrounding ocean waters. Records revealed by rocks indicate to geologists a total of at least four successive submersions and emersions. Undoubtedly, considering our planet's age of several thousands of millions of years, the crust of this continent must have come through many varied and contorted shapes prior to a point beyond which its alterations have not yet been traced backwards in time.

Throughout this vast, unaccountable span of time, quite variant configurations of the land mass adjacent to the Pacific Ocean came and went. Generally, however, a wide separation existed between land to the east and to the west.

The western body of land, in retrospect, became known as Cascadia. The area designated by this name extended from what is now the Selkirks to a position some one hundred miles into the Pacific from our present west coast, and from California to the Yukon. During most of its hundreds of millions of years of existence, what is now Vancouver Island remained a portion of this great mass, rising and sinking with it. By one hundred million years ago, Cascadia had become a series of layers of sedimentary sandstones and limestones. George Mercer Dawson, during his geological survey of the Cape Scott area in the 1880's, found deposits of limestone ranging to an estimated depth of one thousand feet. Since all limestone is formed from skeletons of marine creatures, such a depth of deposit would indicate a submersion over incomprehensible ages of time — since the appearance of calcium-bearing life in earth's oceans.

These earliest forms of life to leave their remains as part of what was to become Vancouver Island consisted mainly of fishes, crustaceans, trilobites and corals. During emersions, hundreds of millions of years ago, amphibians and reptiles apparently made their way ashore. No mammals or birds had appeared yet, and it would seem that the giant dinosaur of Alberta did not appear in Cascadia.

Land masses here would seem to have been comparatively flat during these remote ages. Gradually, coniferous fern trees came into being in huge shallow swamps, so prolific that their compressed vegetation left thick seams of coal under much of the island.

About one hundred million years ago, so geologists tell us, pressures from deep down in the earth forced molten rock and minerals up, under and through Cascadia's vast beds of sedimentary deposits. Mountains resulting from this uplift rose to altitudes thousands of feet above their present heights.

Some twenty-five million years ago, Cascadia once more settled into the Pacific. This time, however, much of the uplifted land mass remained above water. What is now Vancouver Island remains as a residue of old Cascadia, separated from the continental mainland by a comparatively narrow channel, and fronted by a wide continental shelf to the west.

Prior to and during this final gradual submersion, primitive mammals made their appearance among the reptiles, eventually to dominate them. Many of these creatures differed so markedly from their present-day descendants that only the finding of an almost continuous series of remains has made possible the tracing of distinctive species. Primitive forms of not only the bison, musk-ox, deer, and wolf, but also of the horse, rhinoceros, pig, camel, elephant, tiger, and monkey roamed Cascadia many millions of years ago.

By the time Vancouver Island had assumed more or less its present form, many of these proto-mammals had gone, some southward, and some over a land-bridge to Asia. It is a rather intriguing speculation that the horse, which has affected history in so many ways, may have begun its existence in North America, a land its species was not to

2

see again until only a few hundred years ago; and that the camel, which continues to influence cultures in Africa and Asia, is quite possibly of this continent.

For millions of years, the remnants of Cascadia apparently offered an equitable climate for these ancestors of modern mammals; and the country in general offered ample food over great areas of rolling grassland below the mountain peaks of the Eocean upheavals.

Then, for reasons which seem to have followed no discernible pattern, new pressures developed along the entire Pacific coast of North America. Lateral thrusts, although apparently having little effect on Vancouver Island geologically, pushed up whole new mountain ranges to the east, principally the Rocky Mountains.

By some five million years ago, these up-thrusts had reached such altitudes that mountain peaks began to gather snow in accumulating depths. Presence of these ranges, then, contributed to the formation of a series of glacial epochs. The onset of the first of these, along with other factors, no doubt, led either to the appearance of new mammals or to the modification of existing species. The comparatively hairless elephant quite likely evolved into the mastadon and the mammoth, and the rhinoceros acquired a coat of wool. Many mammoth bones have been uncovered in Alaska, and fragments of these ice-age creatures have been found as far south as the Gulf Islands of British Columbia.

Deer and elk, native to Vancouver Island, became larger, possibly attaining their present characteristics. The beaver, also indigenous to the Island, appears to have grown to giant proportions. Skeletal remains found in some sites in North America indicate existence of beavers as large as the present-day black bear. Although no physical remains of such creatures have been found west of the Rockies, legends of giant beaver do persist throughout much of British Columbia. The native people of Sechelt, for instance, retain a vague story of a giant beaver which once, ages ago, made its home on Texada Island. Quite possibly this creature once inhabited the northern end of Vancouver Island also, where beavers are to be found to this day. The possibility is now being considered by some biologists that fluctuations in the size of the elephant, beaver, tiger, and other creatures which attained bulks much in excess of present-day members of the species may be attributed to changes in solar radiation as the earth's magnetic poles shifted. Such a theory is obviously complicated by the fact that not all creatures changed in the same direction, but it could help account for the appearance and the disappearance of a tremendous number of species.

3

Cape Scott, far from the island's high mountain peaks to the south, and separated from the mainland by Queen Charlotte Sound, apparently escaped the succession of Cordilleran ice sheets which alternately formed and melted during the next few million years. Since mean temperatures during glacial epochs were apparently little lower in unglaciated areas than those of today, animals such as the deer, elk, beaver, racoon, mink, and marten may have found conditions on the northern tip of Vancouver Island quite amenable during the past several millions of years.

These conditions would have also proved amenable to human life, at whatever time it may have appeared at this locality. Herein lies one of the abiding mysteries of this continent: When did mankind appear in North America?

In order to put the "discovery" of the Americas in perspective, we must first consider the very origins of the human race. If we believe that humanity appeared in more than one locality, then it is possible that North America is one of mankind's original homes, and "discovery" of its geographic features would have come about from some "cradle of mankind" located on this land mass itself. If, on the other hand, all of mankind has sprung from but one birthplace, then we must consider the location of this birthplace, whether it be somewhere in the "Old" World or in the "New".

At the moment, the hinterland of Tanganyika, unknown to the "Old" World until the middle of the nineteenth century, has produced the oldest remains showing human characteristics. According to analyses of finds made there by the Leakys, humanoid beings were making stone tools almost two million years ago.

The disclosure of a family cave during excavations for an apartment block in Nice, France, has revealed signs of human occupancy dating back some two to three hundred thousand years.

Between these two very remote epochs, a vast gulf of time is spanned by few bridges, and from even the more recent one onward, little is known until some twenty thousand years ago, when Paleolithic Man was leaving his paintings, his tools, and his skeletal remains in caves bordering the Mediterranean. We do not, then, find widespread signs of humanity in either Africa, Asia, or Europe much older than the oldest relics found thus far in North America.

Mankind was already constructing homes, making and using implements, and utilizing fire as far back as the last inter-glacial period. In North America, Folsom-Man points some ten to fifteen thousand years old remain the oldest artifacts known. In the mid 1960's, excavations in the Fraser River canyon, under the direction of Dr. Charles

4

Borden of the University of British Columbia, located signs of human tenancy approximately ten or eleven thousand years old. While nothing in any sense approaching the age of African finds has been unearthed in North America, nevertheless, there is now ample evidence to indicate the presence of mankind throughout much of this continent into the last glacial epoch.

By the time the first foreigners arrived to explore this coast, Cape Scott had likely been occupied by humanity for thousands of years. When examination of this now remote area is carried out, something of the extent of human occupancy there will be established.

History is generally defined as a written record of events. What is not recorded fails to become history. Understandably, then, since they did not record events in any manner that can now be interpreted, aborigines of the North-West coast of North America have no history of their own. They figure in modern history, with a few exceptions, only to the extent that non-Indians have written about them.

This situation is unavoidable to this extent. But histories, basically, have not dealt with the aboriginal North American in his own right — have not featured his ethos. Almost invariably, histories reflect the European immigrant's point of view — his tribulations and his triumphs. The native Indian, in such accounts, represents neither more or less than one of the many strange phenonema encountered by the new-comer in this strange "new" land.

When the present-day reader finds, in an account written by a late-eighteenth-century fur-trader, such as James Stuart Strange, or by a cartographer, such as Captain George Vancouver, that he had "explored" a certain portion of the coastline of what was to become British Columbia, he envisages mountains, islands, inlets and rapids being seen by the human eye for the first time. Nothing in the original accounts, or in successive histories based on these accounts, points to the rather obvious fact that each and every one of these geographic features had been known by aboriginal inhabitants over a period of many thousands of years. Often, even the significant fact that the "explorer" was led by native guides is omitted from such accounts.

Archaeologists and anthropologists tend to agree, on the basis of finds made to the present time, and on the basis of current theory, that human wanderers began making their way to the Americas about twenty thousand years ago, when immense quantities of water held in northern hemisphere ice masses lowered ocean bodies as much as a hundred fathoms below their present sea levels. Thus there existed a land bridge from Asia to North America. Scientists also agree, in general, from studies of language and other differences,

5

that migration to the Americas ceased about eight thousand years ago, when melting glaciers once more caused ocean levels to submerge this land contact.

If we allow the broadest possible theory of mankind's beginnings, we could argue the possibility that humanity is made up of many families, and that one family, or several families, appeared first in the Americas. Even the most conservative point of view admits that human beings appeared in North America, from some source, twenty thousand years or so ago. Following either point of view, we must at least accept some roughly delineated time, approximately twenty thousand years back, as the date of North America's discovery by humanity.

A liberal borrowing from the alternatives of these differing points of view yields an almost unlimited number of possibilities as to the origins of man in North America, and to mankind's duration on this continent. What remains constant is the fact that accounts of the discovery of the Americas should read "discovery by Asiatics" or "discovery by Europeans", inasmuch as all such accounts mention the presence of aboriginal peoples.

There have been many theories advanced as to who first established contact with America since the rise of civilizations in the Old World. Word similarities, incongruous inscriptions, and otherwise unaccountable gaps in history have led to some quite fascinating speculations. According to various theories, such historical peoples as a lost tribe of Israel, Phoenician adventurers, and Alexander the Great's missing legions number among the candidates in an ongoing search for a "first" visitor to the New World.

The oldest written account located thus far would seem to be that of a Buddhist missionary named Hoei-sien, whose report of a long journey to the East was entered in the annals of the Chinese Empire on his return in the year 499 A.D. of the Christian calendar.

Tom MacInnes, who had come to British Columbia as a young boy with his family in 1874, learned of the Chinese missionary from Dr. Samuel Couling, in the library of Dr. George Ernest Morrison, foreign advisor to President Yuan Shi-kai, during a visit to Peking in 1916. Dr. Couling translated to the popular journalist from across the Pacific the official report of this expedition from ancient times. Hoei-sien, Flower of Universal Compassion, had made his long journey eastward to spread the knowledge of the Lord Buddha and the Mahayana, the Wide Raft of Salvation, among the aborigines.

The expedition apparently reached as far south as Acapulco, to which was given the name Fusang, the Chinese designation for "cactus". Three monks were dropped off at Nootka, so the report says, to winter there. According to MacInnes, some Nootka elders, as recently as the beginning of twentieth century, still retained the name Hozeen, and used it in their discourses in Chinook with the young traveller. Nootka's magnet had thus, it would seem, attracted humanity from afar many centuries before the coming of Europeans.

Tom MacInnes also mentions, in *Chinook Days,* a memory of the Fair Swift people who, according to legend, appeared in the Pacific North-West before the coming of the last ice age.

At Gibson's Landing, on West Howe Sound, a brother of the author has found, embedded in hard glacial till, stone tools virtually identical to some European finds estimated to be twenty thousand years old. As the tools were lodged in a hardpan formed by an ice-sheet moving down Howe Sound from the Squamish valley, their manufacture pre-dated, or was at least contemporary with, the last ice age. Is it possible that they, and some paleolithic finds in Europe, are relics of the legendary Fair Swift People who, according to MacInnes, "were superior to any race now living in our ply of things."

While a disinclination of scholars to accept the presence of artifacts as historic record is understandable, the rejection of certain written or sculptored remains is less justified. A sufficient number of these remains have been found in various parts of the world to have earned themselves the distinctive name "petroglyph"; literally, "rock writing".

Two quite distinctive types of petroglyph have been located in the Pacific North-West. One kind, very old, consists of engraved figures. The other, of apparently much later origin, consists of a runic form of writing.

A good example of engraved figures is to be found in Petroglyph Park, on Vancouver Island, south of Nanaimo. The hundreds of engraved figures on this sandstone dome were made known to Europeans by the native people soon after construction of the Hudson's Bay Company post at Nanaimo in 1852. The fact that human beings today cannot decipher the writings, and know nothing of the people who created them, does not, surely, disqualify their being historic. Whoever executed these symbols, painstakingly, quite likely using rock to score rock, undoubtedly conveyed in them a message which other contemporaries could understand. This panel implies an attempt, at some bygone time, to record permanently some phenomena of significance. Other petroglyphs are to be found, nearer Cape Scott, at Fort Rupert, just south of Port Hardy.

Runic inscriptions have suffered much the same fate as petroglyphs.

There seems to be a reluctance, among archaeologists and historians in general, to admit the significance of these relics found at various spots across North America.

The closest to our frame of reference in this story are located near Spokane, Washington, not far from the Canadian border. Professor Olaf Opsjon, a translator of runic inscriptions, assigned to their delineation the year 1010 A.D. They portray, according to the translator, a battle between twenty-four Norse Vikings, accompanied by seven women and a baby, and a band of local natives. The quarrel apparently arose over use of a spring which flowed near the inscribed boulder. Six Vikings, so certain symbols have been translated to say, survived the battle. Validity of the Opsjon interpretation is doubted by some scholars.

The Kensington Stone of Minnesota was clearly inscribed, with Latin words as well as Nordic runes, as a permanent record of a series of tragedies suffered by another band of Europeans who roamed North America hundreds of years before "historic" times. Whereas such terms as "Piltdown Man" continue to occupy space in books published long after they were proved erroneous, general reference books avoid reference to either the petroglyphs or the runic inscriptions as historic communications from the past.

Another sort of inscription used by peoples of past ages, and left for students of archaeology to puzzle over, is the pictograph; that is, "picture writing". Pictographs, or, as they are more commonly known, rock paintings photographed by the author in Sechelt and Jervis Inlets reveal symbols virtually identical to symbols portrayed in ancient Ur, Susa and Luristan, as far back as 3000 B.C. Similar figures include the Tree of Life, the animal walking erect, the double-headed Serpent enclosing a mountain-goat, and the Hebrew menorah. The age of these North-West paintings cannot be determined; the fact that they pre-date the appearance of the first Europeans to have entered these inlets, and that the aboriginal inhabitants would hardly have acquired the symbols from casual voyagers, signifies some body of mythology and legend common to the "Old" World and the "New" stretching back uncounted ages before history, as we now define the term, caught up with and recognized the existence of this continent.

The Pacific North-West, unknown to civilizations of Europe, constituted, over a period of perhaps thousands of years, a Way of Light, which saw one people after another move through its Fertile Crescent from one cultural centre to another.

Frictions and conflicts must have arisen, but stories preserved by coastal peoples make little reference to intertribal strife until after the arrival of Europeans provided commercial competition, alcohol, and weapons. The body of myths and legends identical to or reminiscent of earliest known folk-lore from the Mediterranean and from the south of Asia suggest a long-maintained era of comparative tranquility here, conducive to the perpetuation of beliefs remembered from a now-unknown past. Perhaps there was even continued contact with other parts of the world.

The westward-pointing finger of Cape Scott must have missed some of this ebb and flow of humanity, but it must also have seen its share of land and sea voyagers. Only exhaustive digging can indicate whether or not humanity occupied this area as far back as the time of the "Fair Swift People". The roving Vikings of a thousand years ago, even granting they reached the west coast of North America, would not likely have made their way to this spot — it was left for a band of nineteenth-century Vikings to do so.

Expeditions such as that of Hoei-sien, sailing as they undoubtedly did from headland to headland, would most likely have seen Cape Scott, and would also most likely have been seen by its inhabitants, even if the missionary did not land there.

Many studies have been made, by noted anthropologists, on movements of peoples and adventurous sea-voyages which, it is believed, occurred in the South Pacific at about the time of the eleventh and twelfth centuries of the Christian calendar. Most scientists have sought evidence of influence of peoples of the South Pacific Islands from the East Indies and from South-East Asia. Not until the middle of the twentieth century did Thor Heyerdahl show that such attempts had proved unsuccessful because prevailing winds and ocean currents would have made travel eastward between the tropics literally impossible. Studies made by Heyerdahl and by other members of the Kon-Tiki expedition reveal in abundant detail the feasibility of navigation, not only from Peru to South Pacific archipelagos, but also back to South America from these same islands, through a circuitous route into the belt of westerly winds.

Thor Heyerdahl also discovered, though, from research both throughout the Pacific and on our coast, that many of the most spectacular similarities indicate a relationship eastward, not only to Peru but also to British Columbia.

This renowned and venturesome anthropologist began his search through his curiosity as to the identity of Kane, who, according to Hawaiian legend, had made his way there from the east. References to this culture-hero ancestor invariably, Heyerdahl found, associated his name with a mysterious strait known to the Polynesians as Hakai.

Searching far and wide for such a piece of water, the explorer found it on the British Columbia coast, leading from the Bella Coola Valley westwards toward Cape Scott. At this cape, he also found his mythological Kane.

George Mercer Dawson, one of Canada's most prolific writers in the fields of geology and anthropology, had noted, during a study of the Kwakiutls of northern Vancouver Island in the year 1887, repeated references to a culture-hero whom they called Kan-e-a-ke-luh. Finding that stories of this divine ancestor centered chiefly at Cape Scott, Dawson assumed this locality to be the site of the earliest home of the Nahwittis.

Kan-e-a-ke-luh, the Nahwittis told Dawson, had reached the Northwest Indians, not from across the ocean, but by travelling by land on foot. Finally, after a sojourn at Cape Scott, during which time he performed many miraculous acts, transforming misshapen creatures into the present human form, this spirit-man had continued his journey westward, across the ocean, leaving a brother to remain among the people. Of the presence of this cultural hero in Nahwitti lore, Dawson said:

> A high rock on the coast opposite the end of Nahwitti Bar is said to represent a man who was changed into stone by Kan-e-a-ke-luh, during his journey, for some misconduct. The natives now throw an offering toward this rock in passing, and address some words to it, asking for favorable weather. In the little bay immediately to the east of Cape Scott is a flat greenstone boulder, on the beach, upon which is a natural depression closely resembling in form and size the print of a left foot. This is said to have been made by Kan-e-a-ke-luh when still a mere boy, and the Indians say that the other end of the stride — a right foot mark — is to be seen on Cox Island. No one dares to put his foot on either of these marks, as it is certain to result in misfortune or death.

According to the Kwakiutls, Kane (as the name would appear, shorn of suffixes) gave fire to the Indians, because of which deed the sun was forever said to represent him. In Hawaiian and Maori aboriginal mythologies, Kane represented the sun and, through the sun, light. But since, in Polynesia, light also symbolized knowledge, so did Kane symbolize knowledge, or wisdom. To the aboriginal Kwakiutl, too, then, it is quite possible that the legendary Kane represented not only light but also supreme wisdom.

Along the Pacific North-West coast, the term Kane was by no means restricted to the Kwakiutls. Far to the south of these people,

10

the Sechelts named the condor Tchass-Kane. As a physical entity, Tchass-Kane represented a benefactor to the hunter by circling the elusive mountain goat, thus indicating its whereabouts. As a mythological symbol, Tchass-Kane represented the mind; the "eye of the hand", which must at all times act counter to the base passions' destructive forces. The Sechelt medicine-man drew his power and his wisdom from the sun, as quite likely did other medicine-men along the British Columbia coast.

Now, as has already been mentioned here, there are many myths and legends throughout the Pacific North-West identical to, and many more nearly identical to myths and legends of ancient Egypt, Greece, and the empires of the Tigris-Euphrates. Pictographs in Sechelt and Jervis Inlets, many, located in sheltered niches, still quite clear, reveal symbols identical to symbols portrayed in relics found in ancient Ur, Süsa, and Luristan. The Old Testament, a history of the family of Abraham, who set out, five thousand years ago, from Ur of the Chaldeas, records, among other events, the slaying of Abel by his brother Cain.

If other myths and legends could somehow or other travel half way round the globe thousands of years ago, to be preserved in British Columbia to the present day, is it not possible that the Kane of the Pacific North-West, of Hawaii, and of Polynesia, is directly related to the Cain of ancient Ur? If so, is it not equally possible that the account in Genesis, written when the event was already from a past veiled by time, confuses allegory with fact? If we follow the clue back into the past, we find, not a mortal Cain who slew his brother, but a divine Cain whose teachings replaced earlier beliefs. The existence of similar symbols with differing names can obviously be attributed to coincidence, but surely the existence of similar symbols involving identical names cannot be discredited out of hand.

Who, then, was the Kan-e-a-ke-luh who, ages ago, appeared at Cape Scott to leave with a people, so the legend says, already living there, belief in a divinity inherent in light; in wisdom? If a shadowy memory of Hoei-sien and his Wide Raft of Salvation could, despite only a single brief contact with it, survive at Nootka over a period of fifteen hundred years, is it not possible that the story of Kane, who appeared on foot at Cape Scott, refers to some specific person, or persons, who visited that spot unknown ages ago?

Again, the fact that the event, whenever it may have taken place, was not recorded in what is known as history should not be allowed to detract from the possibility that such a visit may have taken place. The Kwakiutl legends pertaining to Kane are not necessarily less

11

accurate than much of the phenomena written for posterity by Herodotus and other historians. Perhaps, if enough patient investigation were to be applied to the search, answers to such questions as the identity of globe-encircling Kane may some day be found.

CHAPTER II

There is no need, in a story of Cape Scott, to dwell on the search for Cathay, with consequent sightings of and visits to the Pacific North-West in general. Many detailed first-hand accounts of such visits exist, and many investigations of these accounts have subsequently been undertaken. One of the most recent of these, with much modern story added, is Major George Nicholson's *West Coast*, published in 1962. *West Coast* records aboriginal and pioneer stories investigated and observed by the author during many years spent along this unique coastline. Major Nicholson's accounts of pioneer settlements end at Quatsino, the point beyond which the story of the Cape Scott settlements begins.

Some mention, however, must be made of a few trader-explorers who visited the northern extremities of Vancouver Island just prior to and immediately following Captain James Cook's voyage of 1778, which revealed the abundance of sea-otter pelts here.

In 1786, Captain James Hanna, on his second voyage to the West Coast, named an open bay, situated some four leagues below the island's northern tip, St. Patrick's Bay. He also named a cove, located at the upper extremity of this bay, after his vessel, the *Sea Otter*. The name Sea Otter Cove, given by Hanna, became the official designation of this appendage, even though it had already been visited and named by trader James Strange.

The indentation named St. Patrick's Bay by Captain Hanna appeared on a map prepared in 1791 by Commander Francisco Eliza, who had sailed north in 1790 to reoccupy Nootka for Spain, as Bahia de San Josef. The Anglicized version of Commander Eliza's designation for this bay was retained on Admiralty charts.

Strange, trading for the East India Company, had left Bombay in the spring of 1786 with two vessels, the *Captain Cook,* of 300 tons, and a complement of 70, under command of Captain Henry Lowrie; and the *Experiment,* of 100 tons, and 35 men, under Captain Guise. At Nootka, where the vessels arrived in June, Strange permitted Dr. John McKay, surgeon of the expedition, to remain for a time with Chief Maquinna to recover his health and to study the native language and customs.

On August 1, the trader arrived at what he first took for a westernmost promontory of the continent. Off this point, he sighted a chain of seven islands, which he believed had not yet been given names. Concerning this sighting, James Strange wrote in his Journal:

> *This being our first discovery during the expedition, it naturally followed that I should give them a name whereby they may hereafter be known. I accordingly named them after the Patron of this Expedition, my most respected Friend, Mr. David Scott.*

Rounding the cape, to which the same name as that of the island chain became attached, the trader, in a longboat, guided by four native Indians, made his way some leagues down the eastern coastline. Finally, landing on a beach in which he called Whale Bay, on what is now Nigei Island, he climbed a hilltop to obtain a further view. Perceiving that the channel continued as far as the horizon southwards, Strange reasoned it to be the strait said to have been discovered many years previously by Admiral de Fonte. He named this water Queen Charlotte Sound, after the Queen Consort of his monarch, George III. The native people, he found, did not appear to have come into contact with European trade goods, but they seemed to know the value of the iron implements which he gave them in exchange for two sea-otter pelts.

Back at Sea Otter Cove the next day, Strange decided to claim the territory he had discovered for Britain:

> *Before we quitted our present Station, I left many Testimonies behind me, of Our having visited and taken possession of this part of the Coast. In the Body of a large Tree, I cut a deep hole, in which I deposited both Copper, Iron, Beads, besides leaving the Names of our Ships & the Date of Discovery.*

Later geodetic surveys added the names Strange Rock, Lowrie Beach, Guise Bay, and Experiment Bight as memorials to this early argonaut. Whale Bay now appears on charts as Loquillilla Cove. Hanna Point, at the entrance to Sea Otter Cove, and the Sea Otter

Group, in Queen Charlotte Sound, have been added in further recognition of the visits to those places by Captain James Hanna.

Captain Hanna, not knowing of Strange's earlier sighting, named the group of islands off Cape Scott Lance's Island, and the largest of the group Cox Island, after John Cox, who had helped outfit his expedition. Captain George Dixon, in the year 1787, called the group the Beresford Islands. Captain George Vancouver's chart shows them simply as the Scott Islands. All of these names are perpetuated today in the archipelago; and the name Triangle Island was added on the Admiralty Chart of 1847, from the shape of a reef surrounding this island.

Thus, through men intent on trade rather than exploration, the northwest coast of Vancouver Island received more European names than any similar portion of the rest of the coast.

Some years before the well-documented voyages of the argonauts mentioned here, and of others from Britain, the empire of Spain had begun to take an interest in the Pacific North-West. Particularly when, in 1763, Britain acquired New France, Spain realized that she must press her explorations of northern latitudes and lay claim to whatever might lie there if she were to remain in control of the coast.

Accordingly, in 1774, the Viceroy of Mexico despatched the *Santiago,* under the command of Don Juan Perez, to examine the coast as far north as the sixty-fifth degree of latitude. Perez conducted a ceremonious exchange of gifts with a small group of Haidas, but did not land. In 1775, Don Bruno Heceta, commanding the *Santiago,* did land near the fiftieth parallel before turning southwards. Juan Francisco de Bodega y Quadra, accompanying Heceta on the twenty-seven-foot *Sonora,* reached at least as far north as Norfolk Sound. In 1779, Quadra sailed north again, on a larger vessel, the *Favorita,* and spent some time exploring Port Bucareli, Prince of Wales Island, and trading with the native people there.

Since Galiano and Valdez doubted the validity of reports by Indians of an inland waterway during their explorations in the company of Captain George Vancouver in 1792, it is not likely that Quadra had penetrated the Queen Charlotte Sound area from the north during his earlier expeditions. Nevertheless, as Vancouver proceeded through the tidal rapids and into Johnstone Strait, he was amazed at the number of Spanish muskets that he saw in various native lodges. Before the circumnavigation of Vancouver Island by Europeans, then, trade goods had made their way, from one native people to another — north from the Strait of Georgia, and south from Queen Charlotte Sound — for these people understood the insular aspect of our

15

great island. Chief Cheslakee told Captain Vancouver that goods also travelled overland across the island between his village, at the mouth of the Nimpkish River, and Nootka.

Undoubtedly these native peoples saw many traders, whose voyages, and whose undertakings, were not recorded for posterity. Until the establishment of posts by the Hudson's Bay Company in the nineteenth century, most trading was done over the side, or on the deck, of the low-waisted vessels employed in this business. Not all goods offered for exchange by these traders, many of them freebooters, were in the best interests of the natives. The coincidence of muskets and poisonous whiskey led to quarrels and raids among peoples who had hitherto maintained peaceful relations. Blankets and European clothing, which came to be admired by the Indians, often brought to villages ashore disease germs against which their occupants had neither immunity nor medicine. Poisonous liquor, inter-tribal slaughter, smallpox, and tuber-culosis thus began, somewhere in the early nineteenth century, to ravage peoples who had survived the stern natural elements of the North-West Coast throughout untold centuries. Ironically, those who had met and mastered the harshest weathers of the open Pacific, the Koskimos and the Nahwittis, living as they did along the fur-traders' deep-water sailing routes, were first to come into contact with their destructive paraphernalia.

The Koskimos, or Kwisskaynohs, now known as the Quatsinos, so-called from the fact that their aristocrats bound the heads of their baby girls to a rounded taper, were a powerful people when the first fur-traders appeared on the Pacific coast. In 1909, when my grand-father took his family to the northern end of Vancouver Island, they spent a winter near a very small village at Half Way River, on Holberg Inlet — where lived the last permanent aboriginal inhabitants of that water. The head of this arm, where the settlement of Holberg was founded during that same year by Danes from the colony at Cape Scott, had already been long since depopulated.

In November of 1860, when the American brig *Consort* was wrecked in San Josef Bay, Indians still travelling the coast in their native canoes brought word of the disaster to Nootka Sound. Today, there is not a single native habitation between Quatsino and Alert Bay. My grand-uncle, when he settled on the banks of the San Josef River in 1904, found a shell-midden which, so he was told, designated a homesite once called Nohm by the Quatsinos. I, myself, as a boy, on a voyage by skiff to a portion of San Josef Bay known to the settlers as Little South Bay, saw a skeleton, with an amazingly tapered skull, in a skilfully sewn cedar box, on one of the wooded islands there. But

16

of the people who might have told stories of this great open bay, called Kah-cheen-ah by the Quatsinos, with its beautiful white sand beaches and its river rich in fish and wild geese, not a soul remained.

The earliest Danish settlers, around the turn of the century, met one very old native of Cape Scott, whose "white" name, "Chief George", would indicate, if accurate, a life-span dating back to before 1830. This ancient told the European pioneers that he had been the sole survivor, as a very young boy, of an attack on his people by raiders from another tribe. His grandmother had taken him to Nahwitti from his home village, just north of Erasmus Hansen Bay, leaving the site of the massacre forever desolate. In the early 1900's, a few Nahwitti natives made a last visit to this spot to retrieve whatever bones of their ancestors they could find for burial elsewhere. Today, a slowly-decaying shell-heap remains as the only marker of this aboriginal Cape Scott settlement.

The last quarter of the eighteenth century saw Europe paying more and more attention to North America's largest west-coast island. Great Britain, despite intermittent wars with France, and a struggle which resulted in the loss of her American eastern seaboard colonies, persisted in her efforts to maintain a foothold on some portion of the continent's western shores.

Spain, Russia, and the newly-formed United States of America all disputed Britain's claims to any part of this vast coastline. Russian traders succeeded in maintaining their hold on the continental shores and island chain as far south as 54°40', southward from which point both Spain and the United States contested Britain's claims.

Late in the century, Spain made her last bid for sovereignty by establishing a fort in Nootka Sound, and by seizing vessels whose papers allegedly were not in order. Although she never officially relinquished the claims to this coast established by her explorers, Spain did in fact defer to Britain's sea power, and withdrew from the Pacific North-West following Captain George Vancouver's mission here in 1792.

The contest between Britain and the United States was partially settled in 1846, with the continuation of the 49th Parallel westward from the Rockies to the coast as the international boundary. The Oregon Treaty, while establishing a southern boundary to British territory, did nothing to clarify the type of jurisdiction that was to obtain within this piece of British North America. Since 1821, the Hudson's Bay Company had held sole trading rights in what was known as New Caledonia; and the factors of the Company became, in actual fact, the sole dispensers of justice throughout the territory.

In September of 1846, Sir John Pelly, Chairman of the Hudson's Bay Company, proposed to the Secretary of State of the Colonies, Earl Grey, that all territories west of the Rockies be ceded to the Company. Earl Grey replied that the House of Commons would consider such an application excessive, but that a grant of Vancouver's Island would be acceptable to Her Majesty, Queen Victoria, and to Parliament, in view of the services the Company had rendered in holding the Pacific North-West for Britain against American and Russian claims. Accordingly, on January 13, 1849, by Royal Grant, the Hudson's Bay Company received Vancouver Island as a private domain.

One of the conditions of the grant stipulated that the Company was
. . . to settle upon the island within five years a colony of British subjects . . . and to dispose of land for purposes of colonization at reasonable prices . . . If at the expiration of five years no settlement had been made, the Grant shall be forfeited.

The Hudson's Bay Company had already established trading posts at Victoria and at Fort Rupert, and was soon to open a third at Nanaimo. Coal deposits at the last two points were mined, and some farming was undertaken at the southern end of the island. Almost no independent settlers were able, however, to establish homes anywhere in the Company's domain.

In 1858, revocation of the Hudson's Bay Company's grant and establishment of a Crown Colony coincided with the advent of the Fraser River Gold Rush. Governor James Douglas' assertion that gold was to be found throughout the length and breadth of the North-West led to exploration of all accessible territory, including the shores of northern Vancouver Island, for the precious metal. Rumors of finds persisted until far into the present century. One, concerning a fabulous strike, the location of which had been lost, was related to the author in 1930 by an old prospector who still hoped to rediscover the mysterious mine. Black sands, containing extremely fine particles of gold, were discovered between what are now Shushartie and Cache Creek, or Stranby, but the nameless discoverers left little trace of their visits.

In 1860, the Legislative Council of Vancouver Island, in a discussion of means whereby settlers might be enticed to the Crown Colony, suggested that tracts of 160 acres of land be made available to pre-emptors, at four shillings per acre. In 1870, an ordinance cancelling all prior declarations and ordinances made possession of such blocks of land possible without charge, providing that the pre-emptor fulfilled obligations to reside on the property during at least one-half of each year for a minimum of two years, and to complete improvements to his property of at least $100.00 assessment.

With the purchase of Alaska by the United States in 1867, the Crown Colony of British Columbia, which Vancouver Island became a part of in 1866, must have felt itself in the position of a nut in the jaws of a nutcracker. American settlers were populating the northwestern states, and the slogan "Fifty-Four Forty or Fight", which had elected a president in 1844, still echoed across the continent.

It is, then, not unusual that, five years after union of the two westernmost colonies, British Columbia joined Confederation, and at the same time made Crown lands available for pre-emption with little stipulation other than that of citizenship.

The need for immigrants remained acute during the next decades. As gold production in the Cariboo declined, and as other mineral strikes throughout the province proved inconsequential in comparison to the fever of '58, most miners departed for other fields. Even when the last spike of the Canadian Pacific Railway was driven at Craigallachie in 1887, the white population of British Columbia stood at only some ten thousand, of which only a small portion occupied Vancouver Island. However, by 1893, H. M. Burwell, Government Surveyor, could report that a William McGary had established a home and trading post at Shushartie Bay, and that several settlers had made improvements to their properties at the mouth of Cache Creek.

Understandably, individual settlers seldom chose to travel far up the coast from population centres to claim land. Individuals or lone families would not warrant transportation stops. Although native Indians had offered virtually no harm to settlers, most immigrants must have felt some misgivings at the thought of attempting to establish homes along a coastline where almost no other non-Indians lived. At any rate, there could readily be found, along the lower mainland coast, and on southern Vancouver Island, patches of land sufficiently large for individual pre-emptors.

But pieces large enough to sustain a practicable social group, and suited to certain particular agricultural uses, or located near certain specific sources of revenue, such as fishing grounds, in areas not already settled, were not too plentiful.

At a time, then, when the government of British Columbia sought desperately to bolster its infinitesimal European population, certain peoples of European extraction were seeking to establish settlements within which, while complying with citizenship requirements of their new country, they could enjoy a certain measure of self-government and could to a certain extent carry on their own cultural identities.

The solution resorted to, strange as it may seem today, followed the age-old custom of establishing colonies. But, whereas traditional colonies were planted by mother countries in outlying pieces of their empires, the method resorted to in British Columbia involved establishment of colonies within the homeland from countries other than Britain. Thus, under the aegis of the federal and provincial governments, ethnic groups from various countries made their way to the Pacific North-West.

In 1891, a group of Norwegians settled near the lodges of the remnants of the Quatsinos, their settlement taking its name from that of the once-powerful native people.

In 1894, the Reverend Christopher Saugstad, of Crookston, Minnesota, through his correspondence with The Honorable James Baker, Minister of Immigration at Victoria, instigated an Order-in-Council giving permission for a group of persons of Norwegian descent to settle in the Bella Coola Valley. A copy of an indenture forwarded to the Reverend Saugstad from the Minister laid down rules by which title to parcels of one hundred and sixty acres of land could be obtained by individuals or heads of families.

The settlement of Hagensborg, several miles up-river from the present village of Bella Coola, came into existence through the rather strict regulations of this indenture. Descendants of some of the founding families, Saugstads, Gordens, and others, still live in the Bella Coola Valley.

Finlanders, searching for their own special kind of Utopia, established the settlement of Sointula on Malcolm Island. Despite many setbacks, the community still survives, a unique experiment even along the Pacific North-West coast, where the unusual is commonplace.

H. M. Burwell, Government Surveyor, reported favorably on the northern end of Vancouver Island as a potential settlement area in his 1893 report to The Honorable F. G. Vernon, Chief Commissioner of Lands and Works. Surveyor Burwell emphasized the fisheries, minerals, timber, and pasture and agricultural lands. As George Mercer Dawson had noted several years earlier, he mentioned the possibility of a dyke across the head of Hansen Lagoon to create dairy fields.

CHAPTER III

In 1894, a Danish immigrant, Rasmus Hansen, aboard a small schooner, the *Floyborg,* was fishing out of Seattle, on the then newly-discovered fishing banks off the north end of Vancouver Island. On one of these cruises, Hansen went ashore while his vessel lay anchored in Goose Harbor and, in search of ducks or geese, explored the lagoon that lay at its head. There he found a great stretch of tidal meadows, through which ran two streams, both filled with salmon.

Rasmus Hansen conceived the idea that the head of this lagoon would be a desirable spot to start a Danish colony, similar to the Norwegian settlements at Quatsino and at Bella Coola.

In 1896, the federal government published a booklet entitled *The Official Handbook of Information Relating to the Dominion of Canada.* On page 76 of this booklet, stipulations regarding formation of such colonies in British Columbia were laid out:

> *Recent Government surveys have made available for settlement many thousands of acres of Crown lands, both on the mainland and on Vancouver Island. The Minister of Immigration has inaugurated a new system of colonization by the formation of colonies. Two of these have already been formed — one at Bella Coola on the mainland coast, the other at Quatsino Sound on the north-western coast of Vancouver Island. The plan to be adopted to form a new colony is, that when a group of intending colonists agree to form a colony, they must first apply to the Minister of Immigration to find out what locality is open for settlement, then select one or more of their number in whom they have confidence to go and look at the ground, having supplied him or them with*

written authority duly attested that he or they, as the case may be, are authorized to act on behalf of the colonists in dealing with the Government. They also have to produce to the Minister of Immigration a written acceptance from at least thirty colonists that they are ready to accept the terms of an agreement which sets forth that each family possess $300.00 in cash over payment of all just debts; that they will reside on the land so chosen for five years; that at the termination of the said period of five years, improvements shall have been made on the said land to the value of five dollars per acre thereof; that the Crown grant to be given shall be conditional upon the continued residence and performance of the conditions of similar leases issued concurrently therewith, by the other members of the colony to the number of not less than thirty, it being the intention that the colony shall be at least of a number not less than thirty at the conclusion of the period of five years after the date of the issue of the Crown grants. The Government will send a surveyor with the delegates to locate and subdivide the lands. When this is finished, the settlers come in and the Government employs them at wages to build a road through their settlement. The Government, it will thus be seen, makes a free grant of land on condition of its development. It also makes roads and provides schools, but gives no grant of money, either for travelling expenses or any other purpose not mentioned in the agreement. The settlers are expected to have means of their own and will not be nursed in any way . . .

It is quite possible that Rasmus Hansen, before or after his trip ashore, obtained a copy of the 1893 Crown Lands Surveys for British Columbia, and that he read Surveyor Burwell's report on the northern end of Vancouver Island. He undoubtedly knew of the colonies begun at Quatsino and Bella Coola.

Three other interested prospective colonists, Y. Chris Jensen, Peter Thomsen, and Nels C. Nelson, made their way to the lagoon, and liked what they saw. In May of 1896, the four voyagers wrote the following letter to the Honorable James Baker, Minister of Immigration, Victoria, British Columbia:

Dear Sir:

We, the undersigned intending settlers, who have been at Cape Scott looking for land suitable to start a colony on, promise to form a colony of at least 75 settlers in Townships 41, 42, 43 and 44, Rupert District, Vancouver Island, on the terms given page 76 "Official Handbook of Information Relating to the Dominion of

Canada, January, 1896," providing the Government will build:

1. a road from Fisherman's Cove to Sea Otter Cove, with branches to Goose Harbor and the mouth of San Josef River. The latter to be extended along same river to eastern line of Township 41.
2. A dyke at Goose Harbor to protect the lowlands in Township 43 from the tidewater.
3. Two schools for the colony and provide teachers for same.

The work to be carried out this way:

The land to be opened for settlement when at least 15 settlers are ready to go and settle on it, and at least 15 more have signed the agreement (each signature to be accompanied by a $50.00 cheque. This money is to be used for transportation purposes and will be forfeited in case the man does not settle until May 1st, 1897).

1st year. If at least 30 bona fide settlers are on the land May 1st, 1897, then Township 43 and the western row of sections in Township 42 are to be leased to the colony. At least 6 miles of road is to be built during the summer of 1897 (supposed to be from 1 to 2 main road and to 3 branch roads — see plot).

2nd year. If there are at least 50 bona fide settlers May 1st, 1898, the road is to be finished to Sea Otter Cove and Goose Harbor, and the dyke at Goose Harbor is to be built.

3rd year. If there are at least 65 settlers May 1st, 1899, then balance of Township 41 is to be leased to the colony. A school is to be erected and teacher provided, and the branch road to the mouth of the San Josef River completed.

4th year. If there are at least 75 bona fide settlers May 1st, 1900, then balance of Township 42 is to be leased to the colony, a school to be erected and teacher provided, and the road along San Josef River completed.

The colony will develop the resources of the country, especially farming and fishing. The farming will be what generally is termed "mixed farming". The fishing will be principally deep sea fishing, halibut and cod.

We consider the marshy land in Township 43 forms the backbone colony through the first years until the farms can be able to produce and pay. It is with this in view that we intend to start at Fisherman's Cove, which gives shelter for small fishing crafts and is near the fishing banks.

We consider the marshy land in Township 43 forms the backbone of the colony and therefore it is we ask the Govenment to build the dyke for to protect the land, because we have learned by experience

23

*and investigation that to start a colony in heavy timbered land, even
with the best of soil, is almost an impossibility.*

*We are well aware of the necessity of co-operation for the small
farmer and intend, from the start, to have a small steamer or steam
schooner of our own to carry colonists, their goods and provisions
into the country, and fish and farm products of the country to the
market.*

> *Very respectfully yours,*
> *Y. Chr. Jensen,*
> *Peter Thomsen,*
> *R. Hansen,*
> *Nels C. Nelson.*

Colonel Baker's reply stated that his government was prepared to
open the requested land for settlement, free of charge, and to
construct the roads, providing that the settlers abided by the terms
they themselves had laid down.

On July 10, a second letter was sent to the Minister, as follows:

Dear Sir:

*We have now held a couple of meetings in Seattle and Tacoma
and organised a company for colonizing the land around Cape
Scott. Mr. R. Hansen is elected president and Rev. J. Jensen, of
Unumclaw, Washington, secretary-treasurer. Enclosed please find
in translation a copy of the rules we have adopted.*

*While we consider the forest land to be good, we would not dare
to start a large colony at Cape Scott if it was not for the open grass
land in Township 43, and we believe that we should try to effect a
division of the open land in small tracts in order to induce settlers
to come in. Another reason why we think it would be desirable to
divide said land is that it will be of great importance to get a dyke
built at Goose Harbour. All the open land is liable to be overflowed
at high tide, and both the open land and the surrounding forest
land needs draining. If we could get the dyke built then it would
be considerably drier. We believe that if we all help each other
the dyke could be built sooner than if a few have to do it. We
therefore respectfully ask you to inform us whether the Government
would be willing to divide the open grass land in Township 43 in
ten acre lots, of which each settler shall be allowed to take one,
provided he will agree to help build a dyke at Goose Harbour. We
submit the following plan for carrying out the work, but will gladly
receive any suggestions you may give.*

If on the first of May, 1898, 30 of the ten-acre lots are taken up, the work of dyking may commence. If a claimant refuses to do his share toward building the dyke, then his claim shall be forfeited.

All the unclaimed grass land shall be open for new settlers provided they pay the same assessment as those who began the work. This to go to a fund for the maintenance of the dyke in the future. Before building the dyke, propositions as to details are to be presented to the Minister of Immigration for approval on above named principles.

Will you inform us whether a settler can take 80 acres to begin with, and then have his right to 80 acres more reserved.

Further, if you should approve the division of the open grass land into ten-acre lots, how many acres more a man taking one of those lots can take (80 or 120)?

If 15 settlers go to take up land about September 1st, will you send surveyors? Or if the same number gets ready to start before December 1st, will you then send surveyors along to the colony?

We remain, etc.,
Y. Jensen.

Mr. Jensen enclosed the following Provisional Rules for a Danish colony at Cape Scott, Vancouver Island, British Columbia:

The Minister of Immigration considers it most convenient for the colonists to form a company, elect a Board of Directors and enact laws. The Board of Directors shall act on behalf of the Colony with the Government. The rules are submitted to the Minister of Immigration for approval, and if sanctioned by him they will become as binding for the colonist as the laws of the Province. If the Colony is realized, the first meeting will be held about April 1st, 1897, when laws will be enacted and Board of Directors elected for the following year.

In order to further the work, a provisional company is formed, Board of Directors elected and the following rules are in force:

The Board of Directors sets the time for excursions, arranges all concerning these as convenient and cheap as possible; treats with the Government about such as in meantime may occur and which can serve the welfare of the colony; and sees that a trustworthy man accompanies the land seekers. It shall also draft rules for the colony which shall be introduced at the first meeting to be held of the settlers, about April 1, 1897.

Anyone wishing to see the land will let the Secretary know so and, at the same time, send him $1.00 which shall be used to pay for printing, postage, advertising, etc.

To avoid misunderstanding in regard to selection of land, the following rules are in force:— It is considered as self-evident that the men who have expended time and money in seeing the land, shall be permitted to select their land first. Thereafter each one has the right to select his land in the order his announcement of joining the colony was made to the Secretary, subject to the following:— That if one does not go along with the first excursion, then all those behind him on the list, but present then, advance ahead of him and take his place as No. 1 at the next excursion. Unless the announcement to join the colony is accompanied by $1.00, no regard will be paid to it.

A belt of timber along the coast should be reserved, now and in the future as far as the colony goes, at least 20 rods wide.

Every one intending to go out and take up land shall, in a bank at Victoria or some other city on the coast, or in manner which proves satisfactory to the Board of Directors, deposit $50.00 to a fund, which shall be used for means of Communication, a co-operative store, and other enterprises for the growth and improvement of the colony. If a man does not take up land, then he may draw out his money again, but nobody can get his claim recorded by the Government if the $50.00 is not paid in. The money cannot be withdrawn before the colony is approved by the Government and the depositor receives a deed of his land. If a person leaves the colony or fails to comply with the requirements of the Government, then he shall not be entitled to his deposit. The money is considered as shares invested in the enterprises, which shall, as far as possible, pay 5% on the capital invested. This rule shall be incorporated in the rules for the colony, and cannot be altered or abolished before the required five years have elapsed. We maintain this as a guarantee that the individual beginners shall not be left in the cold by the speculators.

Colonel Baker replied that, should the required number of 30 settlers be obtained, the Government would be willing to plot out the land in 10-acre lots at Goose Harbour — that is, at the head of Hansen Lagoon, which ran inland toward Fisherman's Cove, or Bay, from Goose Harbour — and to grant one lot to each settler who helped build a dyke to the satisfaction of the Chief Commissioner of Lands and Works, and to grant each settler an additional 80 acres of land beyond the dyked flats. The Government, he stated, had no objection to the rules laid down for the guidance of the Colony, as enclosed with the letter of July 10, 1896.

In the fall of 1896, Rasmus Hansen and N. C. Nelson were landed by Captain Foote, Commander of the small coastal steamer *Willipa*, at Fisherman's Bay, where they erected a house from driftwood. Hansen also built a skiff, after completing which, he returned to Seattle, leaving Nelson to winter at the prospective colony site.

The founding members of the proposed colony had meanwhile begun to write a series of articles in Danish-language newspapers published in Cedar Falls, Iowa, and in Omaha, Nebraska. These articles, coupled with meetings held in West Coast towns and cities, attracted a small number of daring souls willing to take a plunge into an unknown wilderness.

These enquiries grew out of a series of events and forces, both in Denmark and in North America. In Denmark, the war with Prussia in 1864 had broken the old feudal system, leaving the country for a time in a state of chaos. During this time of uncertainty, one man, Pastor Gruntvig, had appealed to his people's pride in their Viking ancestry to work together, now that they were free from feudalism, to escape the morass that was threatening to engulf them.

Under the stimulus of his urgings, there emerged a system of co-operative factories for the production of uniform grades of butter and bacon, credit unions, and a rural education programme aimed at improved farming practices. All of these movements were controlled by the farmers themselves. Their efforts were so successful that, in a comparatively short time, Denmark not only became pre-eminent in the production of dairy products and bacon, but also became a relatively prosperous country.

Some young men, feeling that there were more opportunities in the New World than in the Old, had migrated to the United States. There, they had sought farmlands in Iowa, in Nebraska, in the Dakotas, and in Washington.

When they made plans for a colony at the northern end of Vancouver Island, aware of the changes for the better that Pastor Gruntvig's teachings had brought to their own country, the founders structured it as a co-operative undertaking, the principles of which they were to adhere to throughout the colony's existence.

A rather complex design of forces combined to propel these individuals from wherever they lived when these articles appeared, and to impel them across an international boundary toward the northern tip of a far-away island. Propulsive forces involved, in varied degrees from one individual to another, a feeling of loss of cultural identity, a spirit of restlessness for adventure, and either inability to secure steady employment in an industrial labor market or dissatisfaction with the trammels imposed by long hours of back-breaking toil for low wages.

Forces that attracted the adventurous or dissatisfied toward Canada in general included a prevailing spirit of optimism in the destiny of this young northern nation. During his campaign, and following his election as Prime Minister in 1896, Wilfrid Laurier repeatedly averred that the 20th century would belong to Canada. He envisioned a tremendous, vital population, filling every nook and cranny of this tremendously vast domain. Cyclic depressions sharpened a desire in many of those affected by disrupted earning conditions to leave the cities, where living expenses remained comparatively high, for the country, where a family could, so it was dreamed, "live off the land".

Prospective immigrants were attracted to Cape Scott by a number of forces. The articles written by Rasmus Hansen and his colleagues painted a picture of an idyllic settlement. Ninety acres of land, ten of natural meadow and eighty of bush or timber, could be had for nothing more than some work spent on improving it. Waters teemed with fish, ducks, and geese; and the land was plentifully supplied with deer. Above all, the colonist could find independence; freedom from the punch-card of mine and mill; opportunity to set his stamp on a new society in a new, untouched land.

So, in March of 1897, the first expedition to the northern end of Vancouver Island set out. Following the co-operative principle, Rasmus Hansen had acquired ownership of the *Floyborg*. This vessel, he thought, would give the settlers opportunity to obtain cash returns from halibut fishing on the nearby banks. It would also serve as a supply ship when required. While the main body of founding colonists, along with Surveyor Ernest Cleveland, were travelling up the inner passage, aboard the chartered *Willipa*, Hansen, Niels Jensen, N. P. Jensen's brother Lars, and Chris Jensen — all experienced men in the handling of sailing vessels, with Jens and Niels Nelson, sailed the schooner in the open Pacific along the island's west coast.

In stormy weather, the main boom broke off Cape Cook. Nevertheless, the men brought the *Floyborg* around Cape Scott to Fisherman's Bay. There, during the night after their arrival, such a sudden swell developed that they had to cut anchor ropes and make sail. They fought their way around the cape again, to Goose Harbor. There, with no anchor, the crew beached the schooner. It broke adrift, however, and was damaged beyond repair.

As the story has come down, it was N. P. Jensen's son, Lars, still only in his teens, who sailed the disabled *Floyborg* up to the lagoon to her final resting place. The *Willipa* was also wrecked, just after her trip to Fisherman's Bay, but was purchased by Captain John Irving and put back into service.

Ernest A. Cleveland, Government Surveyor, wrote to Surveyor-General Tom Kains, Victoria, in July of that year:

Sir:— I have the honour to submit the following report upon my work during the past four months in the Cape Scott colony.

Acting under your instructions of March 19, I left Victoria the following day, accompanied by one assistant and a party of eight or ten colonists.

After a slow passage of five days, we arrived at Fisherman's Bay, the landing place of the settlement — and proceeded at once to examine the country nearby, including the meadow and lagoon lying one and a half miles south-west of Fisherman's Bay, in order to determine the best method for the subdivision of the grass and timbered lands.

Under the agreement entered into with the Government, eighty acres of bush land and a ten-acre block of meadow are to be granted to each member of the colony who works upon a dyke to its satisfactory completion for the reclamation of the meadow from tide water, and upon fulfilling the conditions set forth in the general regulations adopted by the Minister of Immigration for the settlement of the country by means of colonies. The colonists were to furnish as well all assistance on the survey of their lands, with the exception of one experienced assistant.

The area of meadow lands referred to above was found, upon completion of a traverse, to be much less than was anticipated; consequently, the number of ten-acre blocks into which it might be divided would not be sufficient to grant one to each member of the colony; that is to say, there were more eighty-acre blocks of upland than ten-acre blocks of meadow. The colonists were therefore given the option of a block of meadow and eighty acres nearby, or a quarter section just outside the section subdivided into eighties.

The area of grass land flooded only at extremely high tides was found to be one hundred and twenty-four acres, while the area of tidal lands, locally known as the lagoon, and which are flooded at every tide, is five hundred and ten acres.

The soil of the former area is a light loam, and is covered with a fair growth of grass, while that of the larger area varies from silts and sedimentary deposits to sand and coarse gravel.

The lagoon is covered with water to a depth of from three to ten feet at ordinary tides, and from eight to fifteen feet at the January and June tides, at which time the meadow is also flooded.

A slough from thirty to fifty feet in width, having a good bottom of sand, intersects the meadow in an easterly and westerly direction;

29

and about one mile from the head of the lagoon a small river, flowing westerly through the lands of the colony spreads itself over the flats.

The lagoon was cross-sectioned at three different points to ascertain the quantities for a dyke of suitable dimensions at each place, and upon carefully estimating the cost of the work, the conclusion was arrived at that the large volume of water flowing into the lagoon, which must be got rid of by means of sluice gates, thus adding considerably to the cost and maintenance of a dyke, makes the dyking of the whole lagoon an undertaking altogether too expensive for the colony — at least for some time to come. However, a dyke about two thousand feet in length, crossing the lagoon a short distance above the mouth of the main river — thus avoiding a considerable volume of fresh water — will serve to reclaim about one hundred and eighty acres now flooded at every tide, as well as to protect the grass land from the floods at spring tides. The colonists will probably turn their attention to this feature of their work during the coming winter.

Sections 19, 30, and 31, in Township 42, and sections 23, 24, 25, 26, 35 and 36, in Township 43, were wholly or partially subdivided into eighty-acre blocks; and section 18, Township 42 and section 13, Township 43, laid out and subdivided into quarter sections, thereby providing surveyed lots for settlers to the number of about fifty, while thirty more could locate on the sections outlined to the eastward of those mentioned, and also on the unsurveyed sections to the south and west.

This part of the country has been amply described in former reports, but it may be said here that the greater part of the area included in the present settlement is timbered with a fairly heavy growth of pine, cedar, yellow cedar, and hemlock, with considerable areas of fairly open land covered with light, scrubby timber.

Along the banks of the main river, a limited quantity of very fine spruce is to be found, and no doubt will supply the colony with valuable lumber for building purposes as well as for fish boxes and other domestic uses. Some very fair yellow cedar, scattered over the whole area, may prove of considerable value to the colony, should they be able to find a market for that valuable wood, or find some way of manufacturing it into articles for which there is a local demand. The main river, as well as several smaller streams throughout the settlement, furnish abundance of water for domestic purposes, and one or two good water powers for small mills or other appurtenances of a successful colony.

30

The soil, generally, is wet, but will no doubt be brought into satisfactory condition by drainage of the open flats spoken of above.

The country has numerous small rounded hills, all of which are covered with timber.

Near the shore the sal-lal is almost impenetrable, but grows much lighter as one goes back from the sea coast.

As the past season has been exceptionally wet over a great part of the Province, and especially the coast, it is difficult to judge at all accurately as to the humidity of the climate. From the records of Mr. N. C. Nelson, the meteorological observer at this point, extending over the past three months, and also from his observations during the past winter, it is estimated that the annual rainfall lies between sixty and eighty inches. Vegetables and small fruits were in a flourishing condition at Shushartie Bay when I passed there early in July, and as this is only eighteen miles east of the colony, it seems probable that the same conditions of humidity obtain at each place, and that the same products would grow equally well at Fisherman's Bay.

The colonists not arriving early enough in the spring to get any land under cultivation, and being since engaged on the survey and road work, will not be able to satisfy themselves on this point until another season.

It occurs just here that among the numerous matters upon which colonists in a new section must inform themselves are the quality and character of the products of the land and sea at their particular locality, the demand for those products, the permanency of the market, and the cost of placing such products in the market.

With regard to fish, the supply seems unlimited. The halibut banks just off Fisherman's Bay prove a veritable boon to the Indians who were camped on the shore during the latter part of May and early June for the purpose of catching and drying their winter's supply of Kawash (halibut). Nearly every morning, two canoes were out very early and returned before noon, bringing with them from ten to fifteen fine fish. During eight or ten weeks of the summer, the salmon canneries at Rivers Inlet furnish employment for a number of the settlers, while others catch and smoke the salmon running up the lagoon during July and August.

This section of Vancouver Island seems better adapted for dairy farming and stock raising, together with the development of the deep sea fisheries, than for any other purpose. Two or three experienced dairy and stock men, as well as a number of fishermen, among those now settled on the lands, will no doubt be able to test these branches of work in the near future. Many new settlers from various parts of the United States — principally California and Minnesota — are expected during the autumn, having already signified their intention of joining the colony. The coming winter will afford ample opportunity for the settlers to get in good working order.

It was expected, before an examination was made, that Sea Otter Cove — lying about nine miles to the south-west of Fisherman's Bay — would be the harbor for the colony, but upon looking into the matter, this cove proved an undesirable place for the headquarters of the settlement, not only because the harbor is inferior and difficult to enter — being quite impossible for steamers at low tide — but because of the poor character of the land in the immediate vicinity. It was consequently decided that Fisherman's Bay should be the port of call for the steamers. Shushartie Bay, about twenty miles to the eastward, is the nearest available first-class harbor, and during very heavy weather would be the only place at which the effects of the colonists might be landed in safety. Fisherman's Bay lies open to the northward, and though not greatly disturbed by a westerly wind, a northerly or north-westerly gale may produce such a surf as to make landing dangerous or even impossible. From observations during the spring and early summer, it may be said that from March to November little, if any, difficulty will be encountered from this cause, and that during the whole year there may be but very few days when a boat could not land freight or passengers. Doubtless the colonists will shortly have communication with the coast cities by the inside or east coast route instead of by the somewhat uncertain and boisterous west coast — an uncertainty made painfully real during the past season by the failure of the transportation company to forward supplies at the time expected, thereby leaving us very short of provisions for about three weeks.

I respectfully beg to call your attention to a suggestion which has, I believe, been made before, with regard to a trail from Fisherman's Bay eastward to Shushartie; viz., that a small sum, of say fifty dollars per mile, be appropriated for this eighteen or twenty miles of trail, which could be located along the route most likely to be followed by a road in the future. Prospective settlers or colonists would then be able to get through the large section of country lying between these two points without the difficulties now experienced, and which effectually prevent this district from being carefully examined. The trail would be easily accessible from the *coast, both by way of Cache Creek and Nahwitti River, and would give the colonists at Fisherman's Bay a way of getting over to the inside channel at any season or in any weather.*

The road located during the past season through the lands of the colony runs southward from the landing at Fisherman's Bay about three miles, then turns slightly to the eastward, from which point the trail suggested above would be started.

A road one and a quarter miles long will connect the meadow with the main road along the township line, thus affording the settlers access to their hay lands.

Having got the colonists fairly started on the road work, I left my assistant in charge and returned to Victoria.

It may be said with certainty that if our northern coast can be successfully colonized, the Danish colony at Cape Scott will furnish the proof, as no better class of men for the undertaking could be found. They are, without exception, hardy, industrious and intelligent, and well deserve success.

Your obedient servant,
Ernest A. Cleveland

An examination of his maps and notes shows that the young surveyor put the same meticulous care into the plotting of the settlement at Cape Scott as he put into the Vancouver Metropolitan water system, which he planned and administered for much of his life. The Cleveland Dam on the Capilano River stands as testimony of his contribution to the great, widespread population it serves. Had the Cape Scott settlement survived, some significant structure — perhaps, appropriately, a vast dyke — would undoubtedly bear the name Ernest Cleveland.

The British Columbia Sessional Papers for 1898 reported a population of 50, and for 1899 a population of 90 colonists.

Encouraging as Mr. Cleveland's report and the population figures appeared, one of the factors that was to first alter, and eventually help destroy the settlement, lack of suitable transportation, already made itself felt. Much hope had been pinned on the presence of a harbor at Sea Otter Cove. Since no accurate, detailed charts of this section of the coast as yet existed, the earliest settlers could not know, without experiment, that the shallowness of this cove negated its use as a port of any significance.

Even though Fisherman's Bay was susceptible only to winds from the north or north-west, this flaw rendered construction of a wharf there impracticable.

The earliest settlers, although they very soon witnessed the power of the sea, which almost immediately destroyed their halibut dory, may or may not have known of the toll of ships their section of Vancouver Island's west coast had already taken.

The story of the brig *Consort* has already been mentioned on these pages. In 1892, the schooner *Henry Dennis* was also wrecked in San Josef Bay. Again, there were no lives lost. The hulk of one or the other of these sailing vessels worked its way shoreward through the sands of this shallow bay, until upper planks became exposed at very low tides. For years, settlers salvaged copper nails from the doomed vessel. As late as the 1930's, coils of rope still remained to mark the spot where all that was left of the wreck itself had sunk beneath the sand.

If the open expanse of San Josef Bay presented a grim challenge to ships, Cape Scott was even worse. Here, seven miles of reefs, interrupted just enough to lure the unwary mariner into believing that he can squeeze among them, extend out to the Scott Islands. In calm weather, with careful navigation, he can do so.

But the sea can rise here with incredible abruptness, especially when the tidal current changes suddenly to oppose the wind. The schooner *Louisa Downs* was wrecked on these partially submerged reefs in 1868, and her entire crew lost. In 1892, the whaling barque *Hermit* was lost here and, in the same year, wreckage identified as having come from the sealing schooner *Maggie Mac* was found in Erasmus Hansen Bay. No one survived either sinking.

The colonists decided to attempt to repair their schooner, but just then an agreement was reached with the Canadian Pacific Navigation Company to include Fisherman's Bay in the stops made by one of the company's ships making trips north. Thereafter, for several years, during the Klondike gold boom, such vessels as the *Willipa,* a sailing schooner converted to steam, the *Coquitlam,* the *Boscowitz,* the *Queen City,* and the *Tees* made monthly calls at this uncertain port. As there was neither pier nor float, goods had to be lightered to and from the beach. Sometimes, when available manpower was in short supply, heavy objects remained on the beach during the rise and fall of a tide. Boiler and other parts for a steam sawmill, on one occasion, and a piano on another, numbered among the objects that found themselves subjected to this rather strange baptism. Both boiler and instrument seemed to survive their immersions without undue harm.

C. W. Rasmussen and Theo. Fredericksen dragged their dismantled sawmill some three miles to the Fisherman River with a team of horses, then floated it, piece by piece, down the stream, to re-assemble it at a site convenient for their purpose. A dory, a parsonage, timbers for dyke sluice gates, and the colony's first freight and passenger vessel, the *Cape Scott,* were some of the varied uses to which lumber from this mill was put during the few years it operated.

The first "business" center was a store at Fisherman's Bay, in charge of N. C. Nelson, who had spent the winter there in 1896. Following the colonists' policies, the enterprise was operated on a cooperative basis. When authorized, a Post Office was established in the same premises.

In the summer of 1897, less than two months after the colonists landed, fourteen men travelled to Rivers Inlet to try their luck at fishing. The canneries supplied rented gill-nets and skiffs, equipped with oars and sail, and credit coupons, the value of which would be deducted from earnings at the end of the season. Skiffs were towed to the fishing grounds by steam tugs if the distance to be travelled was great, and fish were collected each day aboard open scows towed by these same tugs. Between late June and early August, the open season lasted from Sunday evening to Saturday morning of each week.

Knute Hansen, one of these 1897 Cape Scott fishermen, returned to Rivers Inlet in 1935, almost forty years after his first venture there, to try his luck during the big run of sockeye expected in Rivers Inlet that year. Seventy-five years of age, and bent from innumerable packs over Vancouver Island trails, the old pioneer fought gamely to finish a season that taxed the stamina of even the hardiest of young men. Sometimes, reliving only his good memories, and somewhat forgetful of all the years since he had last rowed a 25-foot skiff into the wind and tide, Knute would reminisce of his early years on the inlet.

The fishermen seldom fished during the day in 1897, he recalled. Nets were very coarse, then, and visible to the fish in any but the milkiest water near the inlet's head. Generally, the fisherman rowed or sailed into his cannery whenever possible in the morning. After a bit of rest, he spent the day tidying his boat and chatting with his companions. Unlike the time of his return, when the fishing grounds blazed with lanterns — one on each boat, and one at the farther end of each net — all was dark at night during his first seasons. A fisherman had neither lantern nor oil-burning Primus stove then. A four-gallon kerosene can, perforated to form a brazier, served to give what little heat and light he needed. The weather was so mild during those far-off days that no tent was needed on the skiff.

Actually, that first season, recalled by Knute Hansen in such rosy colors, was so wet that the expected run of sockeye did not material-ize, with the result that the pioneers returned to their colony, where some had left families, with nothing to show for their loss of time and expended efforts.

In 1892, twenty-two men made the journey to Rivers Inlet, bringing home between $40.00 and $80.00 each. The next three years remained poor, but in 1902 the inlet gave good returns and, from that year on, sockeye gill-netting remained a main source of revenue.

Some of the early fishermen took barrels and salt with them to the Rivers Inlet fishing grounds. The pink salmon, although a beautiful, strong fish at this time of year, before they began their spawning run, brought almost no price at canneries geared to process only the prized sockeye. The Cape Scott fishermen did not turn their pinks into the canneries, but removed the backbones and salted the salmon "bellies". On their return to the colony, they would soak the fish in fresh water to remove some of the salt, then smoke them for winter use. Venison was also smoked, and pork, too, when pigs could be raised.

When the home canner became available, it was put to good use at the north end. The Fredericksens, especially, canned not only beef, but also cream and butter for export, and goose, with cranberry sauce, and fish, in addition, for home use. Mrs. Fredericksen had learned from her mother the art of making canned Danish butter, noted for its ability to remain fresh in tropic temperatures. Even Rivers Inlet could provide its spells of hot weather fatal to butter produced by accepted regular processes. But the Fredericksen product, subjected to successive heatings, day after day, throughout a fishing season, stayed fresh and sweet even after the can was opened. Today, two generations later, Mrs. Fredericksen's granddaughters are still able to make this exceedingly fine butter.

It is difficult now even to imagine the immensity of British Columbia's salmon runs of not so very many years ago. At the turn of the century, such hordes of fish made their way up almost every stream that fishing for purely local use could not have depleted them. Even during the 1930's, so many creek cohoe travelled up the San Josef River system to spawn that countless thousands of fish wriggled their way right into the forests, up rain-swollen rivulets, to be stranded on bare ground when a downpour ceased. On the mainland shores, cohoe, pink, and chum salmon were returning, each summer and fall, up Burrard Inlet, Howe Sound, Jervis Inlet and Kingcome Inlet in countless millions. Most of these waters are closed throughout the year now to gill-net and seine fishing, and the surviving salmon runs are so small that they go virtually unnoticed.

The Cape Scott pioneers made their way to the northern end of Vancouver Island in part because of the very existence of the unlimited supply of fish available there. To these early settlers, fish from the many streams were as available as clams from the beaches and game from the meadows and woods. No one questioned the colonist's right to take salmon from his nearby stream. My grand-uncle, Henry Ohlsen, built a small cannery at his home just over a mile up the San Josef River. In it, he canned fruits, vegetables, and also fish — fish netted in the river — legally, for some years; illegally, during his later years. During many of these later years, while catching and canning a few of these fish for his own use, he was also, on behalf of the Department of Fisheries, watching for and reporting seine boats fishing in San Josef Bay, beyond the river mouth. The fishing that he and other scattered settlers did would never have depleted the hordes of cohoe making their way up this river, any more than the fishing carried on by the vanished people of Nohm had depleted them. Seine fishing in the bay did eventually, after his death, destroy the run.

So, because operators of large canneries wished to export our local salmon throughout the world, the settler who made his home beside a stream because it could supply him with food must desist from fishing this stream so that the salmon which might have gone up it could be caught far out at sea, preserved in a distant cannery, and shipped to foreign countries. Of course, the settler had a right to join in the chase for the salmon, farther and farther out at sea, if he could afford the costly vessel and gear to do so — if, in other words, he wished to become, and could succeed in becoming, a commercial fisherman. He also knew that, in certain favored rivers, such as the Fraser and Skeena, fishing could be carried on legally, while in his stream it could not. While he might hunt deer, which were scarce, he was prohibited from catching salmon, which appeared in abundance. Some, such as my grand-uncle, who tempered justice with expedience, continued to fish. Others obeyed the closure, and tallied up one more thwart to their hopes of making a success of life on northern Vancouver Island.

In 1899, with the settlement only in its third year, the Government of British Columbia informed the Board of Trustees that there would be no further leases let to the Cape Scott colony. As if a constant struggle against natural elements were not sufficient deterrent, the changing governments of this hectic period of the province's history seemed almost to be consciously striving to thwart the tiny community that British Columbia had helped to found and contracted to support.

No word in the letter from Deputy Commissioner of Lands and Works W. S. Gore gave his Government's reasons for its decision to discontinue the issuing of leases at Cape Scott. The colonists knew, however. They knew that the decision had originated in a belief that if large numbers of some one ethnic group were given exclusive rights to settle some particular area, regardless of how remote or how restricted the size of this area, this group would possibly not assimilate rapidly enough into some undefined Canadian way of life.

The colony had come into being during the regime of Premier J. H. Turner. In August of 1899, Lieutenant-Governor Thomas R. McInnes dismissed the Turner Government and called on Charles A. Semlin to form a Cabinet. This Government, under the sponsorship of Attorney-General Joseph Martin, passed, during that same year, the Alien Exclusion Act. While this Act was intended to prevent foreign ownership of gold mines in the Province, it seemed to cause, or to reflect, an inclination to deter foreign ownership of any kind, including land, even by intended citizens.

Two more Governments — under Premiers Joseph Martin and James Dunsmuir, held office within the next year. With so many changes in office, and so little time of actual legislative session, even the civil service ceased to function effectively. Inter-office memoranda of the time indicate the fact that the Lands and Works Department completely lost track of agreements made with the Cape Scott settlement.

A Treasury Department report dated February 23, 1899, cited an expenditure by the Provincial Government of $3,494.12 on the Cape Scott Colony for the year previous. Population of the Colony was listed as approximately 90 in 1898.

It is rather interesting to note that, while British Columbia was doubting the sincerity, and perhaps fearing the strength, of fewer than one hundred immigrants of Danish ancestry to assimilate, many hundreds of Doukhobors were being invited into the Province, under quite special considerations.

While the Cape Scott settlers were required to put up bonds of $50.00 per family, to pay their transportation to the colony, and while they were expected to build their own homes, church, school, and dyke, the new immigrants into the Kootenays were transported free of charge to commodious brick homes provided for them at general revenue expense. There is no need here to comment on the cost of these Kootenay colonies during the ensuing years.

Martin Jensen, Secretary for the colony in 1899, wrote to Deputy Commissioner Gore regarding his notification. Mr. Jensen's letter reads in part:

I notice your advice concerning the Government's decision not to grant any more leases under the contract between the Governmnt of British Columbia and the Board of Trustees of this colony.

This contract was made for an indefinite period, and as we are not aware of not having fulfilled our part of the contract, this decision came very unexpected. Permit me to state that it also is a great disappointment to the settlers who in good faith came to British Columbia as home-seekers and, having staked their welfare in the enterprise, have spent considerable money and much labor in developing the country.

Besides, we think that any competent party will consider the work of clearing the land ample return for a crown grant. There is no doubt in our minds that this resolution of the Government will tend to check our efforts to induce immigration to our locality.

From the Gracchi of ancient Rome down to the Danish colonists of nineteenth century British Columbia, the story remains the same: a government panics at any plan that would make any amount of Crown land the private property of the common individual.

Mr. Jensen must have known that he was understating the situation. The government would not give the colonists title to their plots of wilderness. In 1896, it had promised, tacitly, at least, to lease every plot of land surveyed within the limits of the proposed colony. It had promised to fulfill its obligations regarding road construction. By denying further leases, the government could hope to avoid having to construct a road to Quatsino Sound, as called for during the fourth year of the colony, should the population have reached a total of 75. The population stood at approximately 90 by 1899, but the road was not built — not to Quatsino Sound — not to Sea Otter Cove — not to the mouth of Goose Harbor. The two or three miles that were built simply extended down-island from Fisherman's Bay to a point at which a right angle turn would take it to the dyke.

The combination of poor harbors, lack of income, and discontinuation of leases persuaded some of the first arrivals to leave the settlement. But the idyllic accounts published by the founders in Mid-West newspapers enticed more new settlers than were being lost through discouragement. The names of those who made their way to the north end prior to and just after the turn of the century read like a roll-call of some Norse saga which, in a sense, their venture to this remote tip of land could well be termed.

Some of the founders—Rasmus Hansen, the Reverend Jens Nyland, N. C. Nelson, C. W. Rasmussen, N. P. Jensen and his son Lars, Theo Fredericksen, Martin Jensen, Peter Thomsen, and Y. Christian Jensen

— have already been mentioned here, and Knute Hansen has been referred to with reference to gill-net fishing at Rivers Inlet. Other heads of families, and sons old enough to claim land, included Anders Hansen, brother to Knute, Mads Peter Jorgensen and his son Axel, Kristian Pedersen, N. T. Niken, Bertel Christian Bekker, Carl Pedersen, Sam Jensen, Peder Andersen, with sons Anders, Carl and Niels, Captain Henry Petersen, Soren Thorp, J. C. Jensen, Theo Holm and his son Jens, Peter Glerup, Jens Christian Hanson, Soren Langeson, Hans Olsen, Hans Jensen, Soren Simonsen, Niels Hansen, Byrge Thommesen, Swend Bruhn, Jens Christian Anderson, Jakob Thomsen, Peter Petersen, Jens Fredericksen, brother to Theo, and others whose names could not be traced after so many years.

The first big project tackled by the colonists was the dyke. The first dyke was built just above the mouth of the Fisherman River, square across the Lagoon. It was built mainly by man-power. Earth was dug from either side of the fill and transported up inclined planks by wheelbarrow. When completed in 1899, the thing was 2300 feet long. Flood-gates, fourteen feet in height, had to be installed to close when the sea rose and to open at low tide to release water backed up in the slough, known as Thompsen Creek, that flowed into the head of the lagoon. When the work was completed, so fact or legend has it, the settlers held a community celebration, which lasted through the night. When they looked for their dyke next morning, it was gone. A south-east gale that had arisen during the night had swept away the many months of toil.

Disheartened, but not defeated, the colonists tackled the task of rebuilding the great wall of earth. They chose a site this time farther up the lagoon, and at a slight angle to the direction of prevailing winds, to lessen the effects of tidal action. Here, they scraped fill from a swath fifteen feet wide beyond each side of a twenty-foot base. The new dyke, completed in 1905, rose to a height well above the highest tide, its sides tapering to the width of a wagon-road. At low tide, a wagon could be driven across the packed gravelly beach of the lagoon itself; but at high tide, the dyke road, crossing over the lintel of the sluice-gates, formed the only link between the meadowlands and the five miles beyond to Cape Scott. Sides of the earth fill were covered with a layer of sod to prevent erosion.

The first dyke was not the only undertaking to fall prey to excessively high winter tides. Some of the early colonists, despite warnings from the founding group, built their homes on low lands near the lagoon. During the next winter, these homes would be flooded, sometimes to such an extent that furniture and utensils would float about.

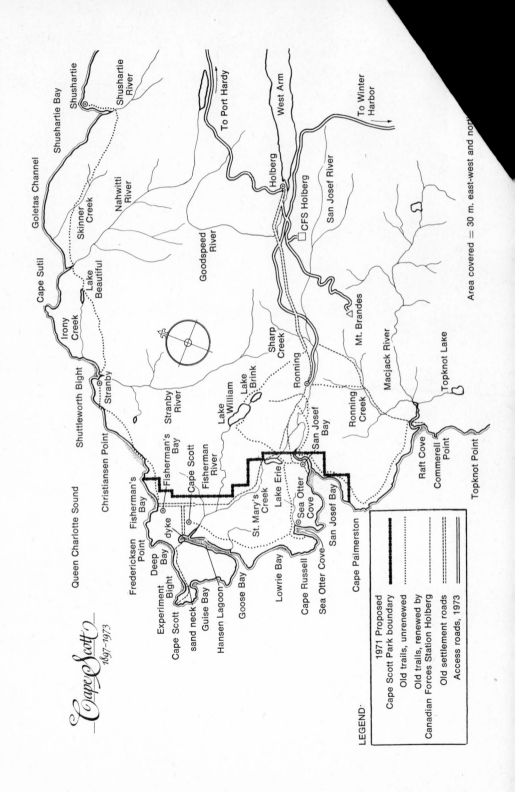

Cape Scott
1897–1973

Queen Charlotte Sound

Goletas Channel

Shushartie Bay

Shushartie

Shushartie River

Skinner Creek

Nahwitti River

Cape Sutil

Lake Beautiful

Irony Creek

Shuttleworth Bight

Christiansen Point

Stranby

Fredericksen Point

Fisherman's Point

Fisherman's Bay

Stranby River

Fisherman Bay

Cape Scott

Fisherman River

To Port Hardy

West Arm

Holberg

CFS Holberg

San Josef River

Goodspeed River

Sharp Creek

Lake Brink

Ronning

To Winter Harbor

Mt. Brandes

Macjack River

Topknot Lake

Ronning Creek

San Josef Bay

San Josef Bay

Raft Cove

Commerell Point

Topknot Point

Cape Palmerston

Lake William

St. Mary's Creek

Lake Erie

Sea Otter Cove

Sea Otter Cove

Cape Russell

Lowrie Bay

Goose Bay

Hansen Lagoon

Guise Bay

sand neck

Cape Scott

Experiment Bight

Deep Bay

dyke

LEGEND·

▬▬▬	1971 Proposed Cape Scott Park boundary
··········	Old trails, unrenewed
– – – –	Old trails, renewed by Canadian Forces Station Holberg
═══════	Old settlement roads
————	Access roads, 1973

Area covered = 30 m. east-west and north

The author's birthplace, San Josef Bay. A C.F.S. Holberg emergency shelter now occupies the identical site.   *Vancouver City Archives*

Last picnic, San Josef Bay, 1917.   *Eva Peterson photo*

Henry Ohlsen's home on San Josef River, 1916.

San Josef Church, near home of Henry Ohlsen.   *Eva Peterson photo*

Jim Cordy's neat homestead, formerly the home of
Knute Hansen.   *Col. J. D. Dickson photo*

Captain Henry Petersen and Mrs. Petersen, 1915.
Photo courtesy Wadey family

J. H. Todd's Provincial Cannery at Rivers Inlet provided summer employment for many Cape Scott settlers 1917 to 1937. *Vancouver City Archives*

Holberg in the early 1920's. *Ashby photo*

Ben Luding's cabin near Lake William, Cape Scott.   *Roland Spencer photo*

Looking northeast from the dyke over portion of dyked land at head of the lagoon.   *Roland Spencer photo*

Hauling hay in home-made solid wheel wagon at the sand neck. *Photo courtesy Fredericksen family*

Nahwitti in the 1870's.

Looking out to Queen Charlotte Sound. In foreground part of sand neck temporarily reclaimed by N. P. Jensen, about 1910.
Photo courtesy Fredericksen family

Sand dunes at the sand neck near the Fredericksens' home. When N. P. Jensen left the sand neck, his fence fell into disrepair and the sand took over. *Photo courtesy Fredericksen family*

The Black Barnacle anchored off the sand neck. In 1938 Lars and Hans
Fredericksen were lost at sea when craft went down in a sudden storm.
Photo courtesy Fredericksen family

Alfred Spencer lived here at the head of the lagoon from 1912 to 1958.
Photo courtesy Fredericksen family

Some of the early Cape Scott Danish pioneers. N. C. Nelson, one of the founders, centre, bareheaded.   *Valborg Johansen photo*

A typical tow of skiffs to the fishing grounds, early 1920's.
Philip Fletcher photo

Not as much damage was done to some of these homes as might be imagined today. The furnishings that floated were as often as not home-made. Since the climate was wetter than was considered suitable for successful sheep raising, wool for blankets was hard to come by. The settlers soon remedied this lack by both hunting wild geese and raising tame ducks and geese. Feather quilts became standard bedding at Cape Scott.

Some colonists built their homes of logs. Some laboriously whipsawed timbers and boards. Most, however, made use of split cedar, the basic architectural material of the aboriginal Indians. Paint was a luxury none could afford. No one with affluence went to Cape Scott in 1900, where every man, regardless of means, must wrest his livelihood from a wilderness perpetually difficult to overcome.

In 1899, in accordance with their original agreement, the colonists negotiated with the Government of British Columbia for a teacher for the classroom in the vicarage near Fisherman's Bay. The teacher decided upon, Karl Brink Christiansen, had known Rasmus Hansen in Chicago, and had come from that city in the company of the Jacobsen family. A graduate of the University of Copenhagen, Christiansen, not young when he made his way to the new land, was respectfully referred to by the colonists as "The Professor" during the years of his life spent at Vancouver Island's north end.

A legend in his own time, "Professor" Christiansen devoted both his time and his money to the young community. To leave some sort of record of the settlement, he photographed its members, in family groups and about their work. He also took pictures of ships that called, and of projects that took shape from shared labor. Unfortunately, only a very few of these photographs of pioneer Cape Scott life could be found by the time this story was in preparation.

In an effort to bolster the school population, Christiansen adopted three young orphan boys. The tragic death of one of these three foster sons, in 1903, emphasized the degree of isolation endured at times by the tiny settlement. The boy, while going about barefoot, cut his foot. Blood poisoning set into an otherwise trivial wound. The nearest hospital, at Alert Bay, lay seventy miles to the south, across seas so storm-tossed that no small boat could possibly set out into them. Despite the fact that the settlement at no time enjoyed the services of a local physician, and that the entire north end of the island frequently remained storm-bound for weeks at a time, no other tragedy similar to the loss of this boy's life occurred throughout the years to come.

A granite plinth marks the grave. The permanence of the stone stands in strange contrast to the fleeting life of the young orphan boy, and of the community into which he was by chance adopted.

Almost invariably, the former settlers with fondest memories of Cape Scott were those who had lived there during their childhood or youth. To the young, not yet pressed down by doubts and cares, Vancouver Island's streams, meadows, wild berry patches, and particularly its sand beaches, presented a natural fairy-land. It was summer camp the year round.

Memories retained from these golden days involved, not the humdrum three R's of schooling, but boat day — the one day a month when, during the first few years of the colony, a real steamer called at Fisherman's Bay. Mrs. Dorothy Petersen, nee Rasmussen, looking back sixty years, recalled the fact that boat day seemed always to be on the 20th of the month. The ship she remembered was the *Queen City*. It came from Victoria, she said, up the west coast of the island. As it passed the mouth of Goose Harbor, the captain would toot his whistle. Its sound would carry throughout the settlement, giving everyone time to walk to Fisherman's Bay to meet the ship. At the sound of the whistle, Mrs. Petersen, first child born into the colony, reminisced, Professor Christiansen gave his students the remainder of the day off to take part in this most exciting event.

In later years, memories of the young retained, not the business of a meeting, attended by entire families at times, as one of the rare opportunities for all of the settlers to come together, but the bits of humor read out from the colony's "newspaper", the *Sandfly*. As recalled by Mrs. Valborg Johansen, daughter of Mads Peter Jacobsen, the thing was not a true newspaper — there were no facilities for, and no demands for — such a publication. The *Sandfly* consisted of bits of news and humor, written on slates at a public gathering, and passed to the Secretary to be read aloud.

Not all childhood memories were joyful ones. Mrs. Dorothy Petersen recalled having to leave home before daylight, during winter months, on her three-mile hike to school, and arriving back home after dark — usually, in steady rain.

To the adult, life in the colony consisted mostly of serious work. The processes of earning a living, building a home, cutting firewood with saws still quite primitive, tending garden and livestock, hunting and fishing for food, with the innumerable miles travelled on foot carrying out these incessant chores, absorbed almost all of every day for both man and woman.

Gill-net fishing has already been discussed. For some families, income from this source constituted the main "stake". Some trapped.

Both marten and mink were plentiful and, in the days before fur farms, heated transportation, and synthetic furs, pelts from these animals found a ready market. Some of the men sought work in the lumbering industry. The job-seekers sometimes rowed or sailed to and from such places as Beaver Cove, where logging and saw-milling were already in operation.

Co-operative undertakings offered some opportunities to socialize. During breaks from their labors on construction "bees", on cutting of trails, and on building the dykes, matters that seemed important to the colony and to the world were discussed. It was for occasions such as this that Mads Peter Jacobsen and others kept abreast, as best they could, with events of the time, and trained themselves to speak fluently in English as well as in their native Danish.

The colonists soon found that monthly steamer service only at Fisherman's Bay was insufficient for their transportation needs. As internal combustion marine motors were then coming into being, they determined to build a craft adapted to both sail and power. Mrs. Valborg Johansen, who spent her later years in Enumclaw, Washington, from where inquiries about formation of a colony at Cape Scott originated, reminisced the building of this vessel in 1966. Lumber was cut, she recalled, in the saw-mill operated by C. W. Rasmussen and Theo Fredericksen, and dragged on a sled by a team of mules to Fisherman's Bay, where the work was carried on in a shed located just above the beach. Mrs. Johansen recalled the steaming planks being fitted into place by Rasmus Hansen, chief builder, assisted by Theo Fredericksen, Soren Thorp, her father, and others. With this undertaking, as with others, Mrs. Johansen pointed out, no one was paid for his labor.

In 1901, with all settlers able to attend present, the ship was christened the *Cape Scott* by Valborg Jacobsen, then thirteen years of age, and launched down the beach. Under command of Captain Henry Petersen, the *Cape Scott* carried passengers and goods to and from Cache Creek, Sea Otter Cove, San Josef Bay, and other points not served by steamers, as these localities began to receive homes along the Pacific and Queen Charlotte Sound shores. Before its tragic end, it was to serve the entire northern tip of the island throughout nearly a decade of stormy seas.

N. P. Jensen, one of the colony's prime instigators, decided that the dairy industry needed to be based on a sound foundation. His wife had learned butter making in Denmark, where the art had been carried to its highest pitch of perfection. Johanna Jensen, when she married Theo Fredericksen, continued the art, and taught her daughters its secrets. Many years after what could be called a settlement had ceased to exist there, Cape Scott butter was still being shipped south by whatever means of transportation was in operation.

Jensen decided, further, that the colony's dairy industry should not have to depend on the manufacture of butter. Accordingly, he brought in machinery for a milk condensery, which he set up near the Fisherman River end of the first dyke. Unfortunately, the colony did not endure long enough to determine what degree of success this venture might ultimately have reached; but his machinery remained even after the pioneer's death, forty years later.

In 1901, then Secretary C. B. Christiansen wrote to Deputy-Commissioner of Lands W. S. Gore, asking if the vacated parsonage, with a suitable area of land surrounding it, could be set aside as a public building, inasmuch as space in the residence had already seen use as school room and meeting hall.

The Danish colonists were independent thinkers, but they were no agnostics. In the town of Enumclaw, Washington, from where the move to form a colony started, churches continue to constitute the dominant buildings. It is likely that the Danes of Enumclaw would have considered a clergyman as essential to the formation of a new settlement as their ancestors had, centuries before.

The Reverend Jens Nyland, then, formed an integral and necessary part in the colony of 1897. One of the first homes built was a parsonage. For a time, this building served not only as living quarters for the pastor, but also as church, meeting room, and school. One of the very first musical instruments brought ashore was Mr. Nyland's portable organ, which played its part in social as well as sacred ceremonies.

The colonists obviously planned to support their pastor. The fact that, after four years of effort, they could not maintain their spiritual leader so destroyed the interest of some families in the venture that they too departed from the settlement.

Deputy-Commissioner Gore replied to say that, not the ten acres asked for by the settlers, but a plot of forty acres was being withdrawn from sale or settlement to serve as school grounds and to be reserved for public purposes.

The irony of this generous gesture could hardly have escaped the colonists. A Government which had, two years previously, ruled that no further leases would be granted to unoccupied lands in the Cape Scott area — not even for lands surveyed by Ernest Cleveland in 1897 for settlement purposes — could now magnanimously reserve four times as much land as asked for by the handful of colonists still trying desperately to maintain a community. Since title to the reserved land remained with the Crown, granting of the reserve constituted no gift whatever; it simply meant that an additional thirty acres could not be acquired for private use under any conditions whatever.

The Government's generosity in setting aside public use reserve did not carry over to a consideration of individual land ownership. The original agreement of 1896 stipulated that those colonists who resided on their homesites for a period of five years would, at the end of that time, receive a Crown Grant, giving them title to this land. In 1902, those colonists who had leased land in 1897 should have received Crown Grants. None did.

Feeling that they would not receive title to their lands in the Cape Scott colony, some members negotiated with the Commissioner of Lands for permission to pre-empt property in the San Josef Valley. An agreement was reached — and promptly forgotten by Victoria. Since this new territory had not yet been opened to pre-emption in general, it could gain in population only at the expense of the Cape Scott colony, with which the agreement was made.

While the question of title to homesites would seem to have been the source of greatest frustration to the settlers, it was not land ownership, but transportation, that gradually destroyed the colony. Water transportation of a sort did in fact survive and outlive what could be termed a settlement on the northern end of Vancouver Island. That it could do so merely emphasized the reality that water contact alone cannot sustain population along the British Columbia coast. Year after year witnesses the loss of such names as Bliss Landing, Refuge Cove, Shoal Bay, Port Neville, Shushartie and others as true ports of call. Of some once-popular and busy stops, nothing at all remains.

A monthly vessel, with no docking facilities, imposed limitations at Fisherman's Bay too harsh for survival. The loading and unloading of livestock proved especially difficult, the animals having to be lowered into the water in slings and then forced to swim. Cattle would swim to shore from the anchored vessel, but they would not swim from the shore out to a waiting ship. Since steamers of those days were not equipped with refrigeration, neither fresh meat nor milk could be exported far enough to reach centers of population on the coast. The *Cape Scott,* although it made trips between Shushartie and Quatsino, could not solve the problems involved in the transportation of perishable exports.

One resource, halibut, which the colony had looked to as a possible source of both food and revenue, was found to be beyond reach. A large dory was built to catch this plentiful fish but, after stormy seas had washed overboard all gear, and had nearly cost the lives of the crew, this venture was abandoned.

Had transportation problems been overcome, land problems could have been solved also. N. P. Jensen showed that hay meadow could be made from lands other than the flats reclaimed by the dyke. At the sand neck, near the extreme tip of the island, he salvaged acres of what had been nothing but dune by constructing fences of driftwood posts, to keep the sand from shifting. The salvaged land produced excellent crops of clover. Almost all of the island between the lagoon and Cape Scott could have served as a natural forage pasture, as temperatures there were kept almost constantly above freezing by the influence of the moderating Japanese Current.

The original 1896 plan, endorsed by the Minister of Immigration at Victoria, called for completion of a road to and along the San Josef River by the settlement's fourth year. Whether or not promise of such a road, giving access at least to such shelter as Sea Otter Cove afforded, represented folly on the part of the Government of British Columbia remains an academic question today. Such a road was never built. Ten years after the colony's beginning, when lack of transportation constituted the main cause of its failure, the road was no nearer than it had been at the end of the second year.

What was built between the Fisherman and the San Josef was a trail. And this trail, making use as it did of trees felled lengthwise, one after the other, over marshy ground, could be traversed by only one means: namely, a nimble-footed human being. Such limited means of transportation could hardly suffice the settlement for export of its produce; even the carrying of only the occasional pack of goods along miles of this sort of route required prodigious expenditures of energy in proportion to the weight transported. Even this trail was not built until after the colony had ceased to be.

The agreement of 1902 had taken some key figures from the Cape Scott settlement. In 1907, two quite unrelated events conspired to completely extinguish the colony. The last steamer called at Fisherman's Bay. Henceforth, the nearest ports of call to Cape Scott would be Quatsino, on the west coast, and Shushartie, on the east. And, in July of the same year, the British Columbia Government set aside a reserve of Provincial Crown land extending from the head of Quatsino Sound north to Cape Scott for pre-emption purposes.

The gap in transportation would be filled, somehow, by small boats. The opening up of the entire north end for pre-emption meant the end of the colony. Blocks of land, within the very limits of the planned colony settlement, which, since 1899, could not be leased to new colonists, could now be pre-empted by individual land-seekers.

And so, reluctantly, the remnants of the Cape Scott colony disbanded. It is easy now, in retrospect, to find faults in the reasoning of these intrepid pioneers. Years after the first failure, when the entire north end of Vancouver Island was doomed to lose a population ten times greater than that of the original Danish colony at Hansen Lagoon, the settlement of this area came in for much criticism.

The Danish immigrants should have realized the folly of their scheme, ran one line of attack. They wanted to found a "Little Denmark", ran another — their school operated almost entirely in Danish, with very little use of the English language. Yet much information persists to contradict such charges.

If there was folly involved, it can hardly be said that only the Danish colonists were foolish. In 1887, George Mercer Dawson had made a comparison of Canada's Yukon Territory and an area in Russia quite similar in size, temperature range, soil, rainfall, and natural resources. While the Yukon held only a few thousand persons of European origin, the Russian province was supporting a population of more than one million. Dawson concluded that Canada's far north could, and should, be developed to maintain a much larger population than it had at the time. In comparison to the Yukon, Cape Scott had a very pleasant climate, and ample undeveloped natural resources. Neither the Minister of Immigration, the Superintendent of Lands and Works nor the Government Surveyors who spent time in the proposed colony remarked on the folly of establishing a settlement at the northern end of Vancouver Island.

As to the charge of exclusive use of the Danish language, the fact that such a charge was not laid during the early years of the colony, when its success seemed assured, but only when the colonists were waging their last hopeless battle for survival, offers at least partial evidence to the contrary.

Mrs. Valborg Johansen, late in her life, commented quite clearly on the colonists' attitudes on this point. Her father, Mads Peter Jacobsen, she said, would read at length each day from some English-language newspaper or periodical during the years the family lived in Chicago. His children, attending school, were expected to correct their father's every lapse. Conscious of the fact that he was making his way in a world dominated by English, the immigrant sought nothing short of perfection in the new tongue. Mrs. Johansen emphasized this point with the assertion, quite startling to her, that her father felt himself knowledgeable enough to argue a point, in either Danish or English, with the colony's intellectual leader, "Professor" Karl Brink Christiansen.

Undoubtedly, the Danish colonists did frequently speak Danish, among themselves. But a rule was very soon laid down that Danish was not to be used in conversation in the company of anyone who did not understand the language. Forgetfulness of this rule on one occasion, through a mere slip of the tongue, destroyed a friendship between one of the founding members and another settler, years after the colony had failed.

Some children, who received the whole of their public school education under the direction of K. B. Christiansen, learned to write quite fluently in English.

The original letter to Colonel Baker, quoted earlier in this story, asking permission to found a colony, was signed by four of the original prospective colonists: T. Chris Jensen, Peter Thomsen, Rasmus Hansen, and Nels C. Nelson. Letters from Rasmus Hansen, Martin Jensen, Peter Thomsen, and K. B. Christiansen, in flawless English, are preserved in departmental files in Victoria. Nels C. Nelson became Postmaster at Cape Scott, a position which involved reading and writing in English. Knute Hansen, who later served as Justice of the Peace, wrote English in an elaborate copperplate. Anders, Knute's younger brother, served as Postmaster at Holberg for many years. Bertel Christian Bekker, a selection of whose writings appears elsewhere in this book, wrote English not only fluently but with an individual style equal to that of a professional essayist. Anders Andersen, who lived nearly sixty years on northern Vancouver Island, late in life prepared a brief to the Department of Highways in support of a road to his home in the San Josef Valley. In many conversations with these and with other original Cape Scott colonists, I used to have to remind myself of the fact that these persons originally had spoken, not the English, but the Danish language.

CHAPTER IV

When the colonists finally decided that they could no longer continue their community against odds which would not let them win, they did so with an almost unanimous decision. By moving to pre-emptions farther down the island, there was a chance that road transportation from the quieter waters of the head of Quatsino Sound might reach their homes.

Some decided to move the entire thirty miles down-island to this spot and to locate a settlement at tidewater there. Quite aware of the fact that this community would have no status as an ethnic community, they nevertheless determined to name their new settlement Holberg, in commemoration of their nationally famous poet.

Others decided to relocate in the valley of the San Josef River, which had its source over the hills south of Holberg, and which flowed almost directly toward Cape Scott for some ten miles.

So a trickle of visionaries made their way to pioneer anew a land to which some had already given ten years of unremitting toil. Few took all their belongings with them. The sawmill had to be abandoned. Stoves and farm equipment, lowered into dory or lifeboat by steam winch during the years that steamers called at Fisherman's Bay, were not easily loaded aboard the *Cape Scott* from shore by hand. And, while the settlement they were leaving had been provided with at least a rudimentary road, the wilderness ahead of them had nothing more than the crudest of trails — much of it, not even that.

Christian Bjerrgaard, Pete Anderson, Sam Jensen, and the Glerups moved to the tip of what became known as the West Arm, and became the first settlers of Holberg, where lodges of the last native inhabitants had already long since disappeared.

Up the Spruce River, now called the Goodspeed, Kristian Hansen took land three miles from tidewater. Along the main trail — as it was slowly hewn out — Knute Hansen re-settled another three miles toward Cape Scott, and, almost another three miles again, off the main trail to the north, towards Lakes Brink and William, his brother Anders took a "claim". Within a few years, Anders Hansen moved to Holberg, where for much of the remainder of his life he operated a store and a boat service to link the settlement with Coal Harbor, and became Postmaster at the new port. But in 1907 there was no port, no store, no Post Office — no village. During the years that the north end could be called "settled", Holberg did not become a cohesive community, even though it grew somewhat — partly at the expense of the area between it and Cape Scott. There was no community hall. No raising "bees" were organized. Men did not gather in "moots" to discuss local and world affairs.

Meanwhile, along the lower San Josef River, another settlement, for a time to prove more vigorous than Holberg, was beginning to take shape.

In far-away Dyke, Iowa, a youngish storekeeper, Henry Ohlsen, consulted a doctor about his failing health. The doctor, diagnosing the symptoms of advanced pulmonary tuberculosis, gave him six months to live, if he would seek out the driest climate in America.

But Henry Ohlsen was possessed of perversity — the type of stubbornness that refuses to accept the decision of death itself. If he could live half a year in the driest climate, how long would he last in the wettest? The wettest was not hard to find.

So, in the year 1904, Henry, his mother, his wife, Emma, and his daughter, Violet, set out for the San Josef valley. Ohlsen chose his pre-emption facing a deep, calm spot in the river, a little over a mile above where it flowed into San Josef Bay.

Henry Ohlsen was not the first settler on the San Josef. The Peder Andersen family, with three grown sons, Anders, Carl, and Niels, had already trekked south from Cape Scott in 1902, and had taken a pre-emption four miles above the river's mouth. They had been followed in 1903 by Axel Sorensen, and in 1904, the same year as the Ohlsens arrived, by Jens Hansen.

Captain Henry Petersen built a second home two miles up the San Josef River, in what was a quiet pool during most of the year. Winter freshets, however, made safe mooring in the river impossible. Petersen then built a third home at Sea Otter Cove, and managed to keep his vessel there, even in stormy weather, until his death in 1924. Soren Simonsen and C. W. Rasmussen, loath to leave the seashore, also moved from Cape Scott to Sea Otter Cove, to make their homes near the spot where James Stuart Strange had placed testimonials of his visit in a hole cut into a tree to substantiate his claim to this northern coastline on behalf of Britain.

At this same time, A. M. Lyon, seeing the possibilities of trading with the native peoples, brought his family to Hardy Bay. There, in 1904, on the eastern shores of the bay, at a site to be known for a few years as Port Hardy, he established a post, at which he bartered goods for furs, with the Hudson's Bay blanket the unit of exchange. During the next few years, a pack-trail was pushed through to Coal Harbor, on Quatsino Sound. Much of the twelve-mile route traversed muskeg, necessitating the laying of "corduroy" puncheon. The corduroy trail, consisting, generally, of four-foot lengths of small trees split and laid side by side, with the half-round facing upwards, was to become a familiar sight throughout much of the island's north end.

At the Coal Harbor end of the trail, the Hole family later built a stop-over hotel to serve travellers making their way across the island at this comparatively narrow constriction. During her family's stay on the West Arm of Quatsino Sound in 1909, my mother walked this trail both ways, before any sort of inn existed at either end.

The trail was gradually widened to a road, and, with the advent of the motor-vehicle, it helped to forge a link between Holberg and the inland waterway to southern British Columbia through a protected port. Today, Port Hardy, as it is again known, after many intervening years as Hardy Bay, has developed into a transportation hub, by land, sea, and air, for the Quatsino Sound-Bull Harbor-Holberg area. Lacking its own road system, the Holberg-Cape Scott settlements, however, received no real benefit from this new route during the years that the northern tip of the island could be said to have been "settled".

After 1907, work did proceed on a land route between Holberg and Cape Scott. Bridges sufficiently wide to accommodate wagons were built across streams, but small crews of men, working without power equipment, could make only slow progress against the rain-forest of northern Vancouver Island.

At first, work on this route was carried on from the Cape Scott end. By about 1908, a trail wound its way from the Fisherman River to the head of Lake Erie. For some years, no practicable land route existed along its shores. Travellers made their way down the lake by an assortment of dug-outs and home-made skiffs to where the trail continued on to Henry Ohlsen's store and Post Office at San Josef Bay. There, travellers took to skiffs again to cross the river. One Government skiff was kept moored at each bank, so that a traveller

51

journeying either way between Cape Scott and Holberg could cross the San Josef River at this point. Unwritten law required that a skiff be left at each side of the river. The conscientious traveller was thus obliged to row across the river three times, once with the second skiff in tow — no simple task during winter freshets. Although most settlers observed the established code, a few did not, leaving others who might be walking the same direction stranded until someone arrived from the opposite way to bring one of the skiffs across.

Near the Andersen meadows, three miles upriver, a giant spruce tree, felled at a comparatively narrow spot, bridged the stream. Flattened slightly, it served for many years as a quite solid and safe crossing — under normal daylight conditions. A freshet finally took out this original huge log, however, and time exacted its toll on at least one replacement. I know that my mother commented, during our 1930 return visit to the north end, that the log we were crossing then was not the one she had last seen ten years before. Of course, since tall spruce trees growing at a suitable narrow spot along the river bank were often some distance apart, replacement of a bridge also involved relocation of the trail at both ends.

From this second crossing of the San Josef, the early trail meandered through the Andersen meadows, and then from pre-emption to pre-emption, parallel to the river, on its way down-island toward Holberg. Because of these perpetual convolutions, the journey from Cape Scott, a distance of thirty miles in a direct line, was made almost half again as long. Because the early trail-makers had no equipment with which to fill swampy ground, they resorted to felling trees, one diagonally across another, to make progress feasible. My mother recalls having had to walk a series of as many as twenty such trunks, some high in the air, during her first visit to the north end, in 1909.

Twenty years later, when pre-emptions which had caused the trail to form a great right angle had been abandoned, an alternate way, along a sort of hypotenuse, from A. P. Andersen's to Ronning, was cut through the wilderness. Whereas the longer route had been made on comparatively firm ground, however, this cut-off ran through swampy river-bed. Thus the early "snake-fence" method was reverted to. I sometimes took this route during the 1930's. The slender hemlock trunks at times veered at such close angles that I had to remind myself at intervals which way I was proceeding, as all sense of direction became lost.

The trail continued more or less parallel to the San Josef River to a point about three miles above Holberg, then followed down the west bank of the Goodspeed. About one and a half miles upstream, a crossing by means of the inevitable felled spruce tree took the trail to the Holberg side of the river, which it hugged closely to tidewater.

Only the experienced walker could make the journey from one end of this trail to the other in a single day. Usually, he did not try to do so, but preferred to break the trip at the home of some friend along the way. Such a visit served many purposes. Each home along the main trail served as a sort of inn, where those travelling by could spend the night. The host, isolated from the outside world between his own hikes to store and Post Office, welcomed any news that the visitor might bring. The visitor might also bring mail, and might take out-going letters to one of the Post Offices established at Holberg, San Josef Bay, Sea Otter Cove, and Cape Scott. In turn, the traveller might exchange roles and play host.

From Fisherman's Bay, the trail continued on down the east coast through Cache Creek and Nahwitti and on to Shushartie. Although portions of this route were worked on sporadically, and short stretches even cleared to wagon-road width, most of the trail remained nothing more than a narrow slashing through forest or muskeg, with little or no attention paid to conditions underfoot. So strenuous was the nine-mile route from Nahwitti to Shushartie, for instance, that a walker could not make the return journey, during most of the year, in one day.

In later years, the Cape Scott - Holberg trail was pushed through along the eastern shores of Lake Erie, and thence, in a more or less straight line, to Ronning. At its final stage of development, a rough roadbed existed from Holberg eight miles west to Ronning, and a fair road from Fisherman's Bay to the dyke across the lagoon. Between these road-ends lay a ten-mile stretch of trail along which a saddle- or pack-horse could be used.

But most settlers lived off this lately-developed piece of main trail — if they had not already left the country before it was improved. They lived along stretches of the meandering old main trail, or on side-trails which led across spindly tree-trunks, over windfalls too large to be cut out of the way, and even around rocky buffs along the west coast's iron-bound shoreline.

Since horses could not negotiate such elusive ways, all goods had to be transported by means of the ubiquitous pack-board strapped to the human back. Flour, sugar, canned milk, salt, oatmeal, and other basic groceries; candles, kerosene, nails, stoves, tools, kitchen utensils, bedding — literally any commodity that needed to be transported — were carried on this universal contrivance. Standard pack for an able-bodied man was one hundred and ten pounds — one twentieth of the old long ton. Each packer devised his own style of board and his own personal method of arranging his load. Some purchased, or made, a board that lay flat along the back; others preferred a model designed to sit along the pelvis and around the hips, like the back of a chair. Most preferred to keep their loads high, but a few, who liked to walk in a more upright position than that permitted by a high load, kept the center of balance near the bottom of the load.

Whatever the style of board or the placement of a load on it, the pack-board user had to re-train his respiratory system. Invariably, the novice would bend forward too far, cutting off his beathing. Facility usually came with use, and the majority of north end adult males — and some females — could carry a standard pack mile after mile, through muskeg, over windfalls, and along the invariable tree-trunk bridges.

My grand-uncle, operating the store at San Josef Bay — the only store between Cape Scott and Holberg — saw, and helped load, an endless procession of pack-boards, with a wide variety of goods. Some of these pack-board episodes, involving exceptionally heavy weights, took their place in the general body of north end lore.

According to one tale, a brother and sister, both very strong, set out from the San Josef store one day, each with a pack. When they arrived at their cabin, several miles up the trail, the brother chided the sister for having forgotten a sack of flour. The sister, conscious of her triumph, threw open the oven door of a stove still strapped to her packboard, to reveal the added fifty-pound burden.

In another story, two stoves, equally heavy, arrived at San Josef Bay on the same freight boat. While one purchaser, built for pack-board work, was leaving the store, the other, Charley Verner, who had lost a foot not many years before, arrived. Despite Henry Ohlsen's objections, Verner insisted on setting out on a three-mile hike up the trail, with the stove on his back. A few hours later, Ohlsen had occasion to set out along the same trail. About a mile from the store, where the shoulder of the trail fell away into muskeg, he noticed a pair of boots lying, soles uppermost, partially concealed by salmon-berry bush. Peering down over the bank, he looked into Charley Verner's eyes. The pre-emptor had fallen with his load, off the trail, and had come to rest on his back, with his head barely above the surface of the swamp, and unable to release himself from his pack-straps because of the stove's weight. Even when he heard someone approaching on the trail, pride and stubbornness had kept him from calling out.

Despite the precarious trails, and the tons of goods carried throughout the settlement's existence, no fatalities resulted from such falls as this.

Henry Ohlsen himself, in 1930, twenty-five years after his fore-ordained death from tuberculosis, could still manage almost a full pack over five miles of trail without a rest.

Lack of a road did help to kill the Cape Scott colony, and would eventually help to destroy the entire north end settlement. In the meantime, however, settlers continued to arrive in the Goodspeed and San Josef Valleys in ever-increasing numbers. If one means of transportation failed to fulfill their needs, another must be implemented.

The only other — the original means — was by water. The advance guard of the colonists had arrived in 1896 in a Columbia River skiff, a vessel altogether too slow and uncertain for a freighting service. The community-owned *Floyborg* lay on the beach. But, when one ship dropped out of service, another took its place.

The colonists had built a number of dories, or skiffs, as they came to be generally constructed on this coast. These small craft saw duty as general purpose carriers to and from steamers, and as transports on job hunting expeditions down the east coast.

In 1901, the colonists built their first power vessel. A camera record left by K. B. Christiansen shows most of the tiny colony present. Thirteen-year-old Valborg Jacobsen is caught in the photo with christening bottle poised aloft above the 28-foot vessel's bow. Appropriately, it was named the *Cape Scott.*

Following the loss of the *Floyborg,* the Canadian Pacific Navigation Company made calls at Fisherman's Bay, as mentioned earlier in this story. When this run around Cape Scott was discontinued, in 1907, settlers had to depend entirely on the *Cape Scott* to carry passengers and freight. The cessation of steamer contact contributed, as has already been suggested, to the end of an organized colony at Cape Scott. Some families, however, chose to remain on their hard-earned homesites. These people were now entirely dependent on their small vessel. The end of the colony did not, then, mark the end of transportation.

But the *Cape Scott,* built to serve the needs of a hundred or so colonists, and not actually required to perform this task while steamers called at Fisherman's Bay, now was called upon to maintain a half dozen additional ports. From his home in Sea Otter Cove, Captain Henry Petersen undertook to fill the gap left by the discontinued steamer run. He would meet the steamer from Victoria — usually, still the *Tees* — at Quatsino, and from there carry whatever passengers and goods were destined for farther up the coast.

After 1907, as settlers began to appear at Holberg, Captain Petersen, with Lars Jensen as mate, added a run through the Narrows and up the West Arm. The little ship was already making stops at San Josef Bay and Sea Otter Cove. Now, after discontinuation of steamer service at Fisherman's Bay, it was required to extend its run to whatever anchorage could be made use of near Cape Scott.

Each mile of coast and each place of moorage offered its own particular problem to the mariner. No other portion of British Columbia's open Pacific coastline has at any time been served solely by a vessel thirty feet in length and propelled by a motor of less than ten horse-power. Today, west coast fish-boats are taken through these waters, but they are usually larger than the *Cape Scott,* their motors are usually more powerful, and they travel only during the summer fishing season. No small craft now tackle this stretch of water during winter months.

Fishermen familiar with the locale can vouch for the suddenness with which even a summer wind can spring up. While the north end skippers of the early 1900's did not set out in the midst of a gale, they were sometimes caught in one. Unable to outrun the storm, they had to endure it — if they could.

Members of the Fredericksen family often saw, from shore, the unique effects produced by a winter south-easter. So solid-looking were the masses of mixed spray, rain and mist that sometimes there seemed to be living shapes moving up the beach near their home at the sand neck. So vivid were the images created by the storm, and so real the old Indian legends of creatures of the deep, that the younger Fredericksens would examine the sands, after the storm had subsided, for footprints.

During World War II, the freighter *Northolm* met its end in a Cape Scott storm. Members of an RCAF detachment, stationed at the Cape, watched helplessly as the disabled vessel drifted near the rocks, then slowly moved out again. To either the crew or the onlookers, any attempt to launch a lifeboat meant death to those manning it. The *Northolm* was never seen again. It took its place in the lengthy register of ships claimed by Vancouver Island's west coast, the "Graveyard of the Pacific".

Every call at San Josef Bay entailed travelling up the river to the boat landing, a distance of slightly over a mile. At low tide the river runs over the lower end of the bay's long sand beach. Not until half tide is the true mouth of the river reached. There, two huge boulders stand guard over the narrow entrance. Coming in at the crest of a spring tide, and impelled by the surge of the open Pacific, Captain

56

Petersen — and those seamen who came after him — had to thread the needle between these ominous landmarks. En route to the landing, there always seemed to be at least two logs half buried in the river bottom — usually, somewhere at the bend. In later years, when Julius Rasmussen was postponing the inevitable end of this run for several years, I have seen his vessel suddenly show six inches or more of her copper paint as it forced its way over one, and then another, of these ever-present hazards.

The Nahwitti Bar spreads out past Goletas Channel, to surround Hope Island. There is no way for a boat to leave or approach the river mouth to or from the north without having to cross this shallow sand bar. Any sort of wind creates great friction waves here.

As settlers began to seek land along the island's east coast, the *Cape Scott's* run gradually extended along that shoreline. Finally, for some years, the tiny ship was picking up and discharging passengers, mail, and freight regularly from Quatsino to far below Fisherman's Bay. It was almost as if Magellan had rounded Cape Horn, not once, but once every week of the year. Internal combustion marine motors were not the most reliable of machines in those days, and the twenty-eight-foot craft was only a toothpick in the seas it traversed. It was a patrol that ran on borrowed time, along a route which seldom relented in its fury, and never in its vigil.

The time ran out for Lars Jensen in January of 1910. In 1909, Captain Petersen had decided to return to his native Denmark for a visit. Lars advanced to skipper of the *Cape Scott,* and continued the runs from Quatsino to Holberg and around the north end.

On his last voyage, he had with him a younger foster-brother, a boy whose hip was crippled. Somewhere up-coast from Quatsino, the *Cape Scott* disappeared.

When the last hope for the vessel's safe arrival faded away, N. P. Jensen, without food and without sleep, walked the west coast shoreline from Cape Scott to the entrance to Quatsino Sound. It is not hard to realize that the father, one of the founders of the former colony, felt himself responsible for the death of the sons he had brought to this strange, hard land.

It is possible that Jensen passed almost within reach of the bodies. Years later, when portions of the coast were travelled by trappers and new settlers, two skeletons were found in the undergrowth above an isolated beach. One was that of a strong man; the other, of a boy, with a twisted hip. What caused the one to die by the side of the other will never be known. But those who knew Lars Jensen were convinced that, even if the storm that sank his boat had taken most of his strength, he still could have made his way through the wilds to safety. The same acquaintances felt even more certain that he would not have abandoned the foster-child, his only brother. Exactly what did occur can never be solved, but enough was found to make the sadness of the loss itself almost secondary to the story sealed within it.

Like a decimated company that closes ranks about its fallen, other mariners stepped forward to take the place of Lars Jensen. Jephtha Skinner, of Shushartie, who had made his way north in 1894, two years ahead of the Cape Scott colonists, took over the run along the island's eastern shoreline. Although there was little wealth in the area, settlers pooled their resources, and persuaded Captain Henry Petersen to have another vessel built — this time, in Vancouver. The new boat, the *Cape Scott II,* made its first run in March of 1911.

In 1913, Petersen transferred the vessel to Walter Petersen, stepson of N. C. Nelson, first prospective colonist to winter at Cape Scott.

Both Jephtha Skinner and Walter Petersen met the fate of their predecessor. Skinner, a fearless pilot, after a string of near-disasters, went down with his boat in the midst of a sudden gale on the Nahwitti Bar, leaving a young wife and small daughter behind him. Adrian Davis took over the run from Shushartie to Fisherman's Bay, and served on it until there were no settlers to serve. Walter Petersen, after having conquered all that the weather could muster against him for two years, met his end in 1915 under rather mysterious circumstances when he supposedly stepped over the side of his boat by accident one night while moored at Quatsino.

Captain Petersen, not young when he had first undertaken to command the *Cape Scott,* fifteen years before, agreed to return to duty on the *Cape Scott II.* During the last ten years of his life, he brushed close to death many times. More than once, on crossing the bar at the San Josef River mouth, he warned his passengers to remove their shoes, in case they had to swim. He himself could not take a hand from the controls of his ship to follow his own precaution. Toward the end, his daughter Nora used to watch for his coming from a lookout tree near their home in Sea Otter Cove. As the boat entered the harbor, she would row out to meet him, pry his fingers from the wheel, and help him home.

When he passed away in 1924, the only mariner of the settlement up to that time to die ashore, he was buried in the tiny cemetery near the banks of the San Josef River. In addition to his years at sea out of Denmark, he had overcome the worst that the open Pacific could hurl against him for a total of twenty years. A 400-pound stone was trundled into place at the head of his grave, where, even a decade later, it appeared incongruous amid a returning wilderness.

Ironically, at the time of Lars Jensen's death, the settlement he served was not the one his father had helped to found. Of the colonists, only a handful remained in the Cape Scott area by 1910. Among that small group still at the sand neck, where native Indians had once portaged their canoes, were his father, N. P. Jensen, his sister, Johanna, and her husband, Theo Fredericksen. When a son was born to Johanna and Theo, they named him after his late uncle. The story of this Lars is as sad as that of his predecessor.

There can be little doubt of the disillusionment felt by the people who, some in the middle of their lives, had set out to make new homes, and who now, with ten years or more added to their ages, had to start once more. Behind them lay their homes, their church, their school, their pasture lands, their dyke — and the spirit that had made of all of these a community. Ahead lay a territory as wild as their former settlement had been a decade before, and the question of what to do there.

Represented by a graph, the line of the original colony would have descended almost to the pre-1897 base at Cape Scott, but that representing the entire north end settlement would have shown an inclination toward continuous increase.

The period from 1909 to the outbreak of World War I saw the completion of surveys of most of the townships suitable for settlement, and the pre-empting of almost every plot as soon as it was thrown open. In fact, a letter to the Victoria *Times,* some years later, when the settlement was making its last desperate struggle for existence, claimed that during this period, all applicants for land at the Government offices were directed to the north end of Vancouver Island. Surveyors themselves could not find sufficient words to praise the developing settlement.

H. H. Browne, reporting on his surveys in 1912, included in his report an account of agricultural fact and potential:

. . . Speaking generally, the soil is a rich alluvial deposit, lying on hard-pan, with a depth of from 3 to 4 feet. This is in the valley; on the ridges and benches there is much gravel, but these gravels are also fertile, as has been proved. Everywhere the soil must be exposed to the sun, and vigorous tillage is necessary; then good crops of vegetables are assured. For example, last year John Laurie, at Sea Otter Cove, on the ocean side, cleared away the weeds, dug up his ground in small patches wherever he could get in his spade, covered it with sea-wrack — mostly kelp — dug it up again, and

then planted potatoes and other garden-stuff. There was hardly an acre in all of it, but he sold to me $77 worth of vegetables for my camp; and still has left forty-two sacks of potatoes and a lot of cabbages and turnips, for which he will probably get 2 cents a pound. Every settler can do the same, but unfortunately every settler has not at present means of reaching a market.

. . . The summers are not very hot, as there is almost always a good wind from Queen Charlotte Sound, which brings moisture with it in the mornings, and the afternoons are rather hot. This is good for small fruits, such as raspberries, which everywhere grow abundantly. The land is hard to clear, undoubtedly, but there are salmonberry patches which are large enough and will yield crops of any sort. Then there is a little grazing on nearly every quarter-section where a man may keep a cow or two. Pigs do well, I am assured, and pork finds a ready market. Until there is completed a good wagon-road through the district, the market must, of course, remain a very limited one. But I am speaking of possibilities.

In addition to this positive encouragement, a minor depression during the pre-war years added a negative factor, which tended to gravitate settlers toward outlying lands. No doubt, some of the pre-emptors were, or thought they were, speculators. One hundred and sixty acres of land, if it could be subdivided and sold, could bring in wealth; and many plots had fine stands of spruce and hemlock timber, which the holders hoped to sell. However, pre-emption laws permitted no mere paper speculation — no absentee ownership — and a man does not generally remove himself and his family to a wilderness such as this for years as a speculative manoeuver.

These new pioneers landed — at San Josef Bay, at Sea Otter Cove, at Fisherman's Bay, at Cache Creek, at Nahwitti, at Shushartie. Their effects landed with them, and the boat that had brought them departed. Between the landing and their homesites stretched a long, thin line of trail, and the only means of transportation was by packboards on their backs.

Some came with a greatly distorted sense of distances. John Harestad, who took land at Sea Otter Cove, could look back on this ignorance of geography, years later, with wry humor. Maps he had seen, he recalled, gave him the impression that Queen Charlotte Sound, which he discovered later to be sixty miles between Cape Scott and Cape Caution, was only a step from shore to shore.

Some, having misunderstood or been unaware of the elemental conditions that were to prevail, arrived with articles of furniture that proved to be incongruous in the setting into which they were introduced. Beds, trunks, and stoves posed their problems, the only solution to which was an expenditure of human energy and ingenuity in proportion to the weight and size of the object. John Buol and his family, attempting to reach San Josef Bay with furnishings that included a piano, were half way along the West Arm before discovering that they could not possibly take the heavier articles over the trail from Holberg. Captain Henry Petersen offered to take the bulky instrument lashed across the stern of his *Cape Scott,* with the provisions that if the west coast seas became too rough he would have to cut the ropes and let it slip overboard. Buol declined the offer, managed to leave the piano with a Price family at Halfway River, then travelled, with his wife and daughters, to San Josef in the little ship. The next year, he trundled the instrument, which had already been transported from Wisconsin, to a new home in Oklahoma.

Captain Petersen did bring a piano to Henry Ohlsen for his wife, Emma, and their daughter, Violet. Later, he also brought an organ for the new church, through the breakers and up the shallow San Josef River.

The passage of time brought surveyors, who laid out the land, up hill and down dale, along beach and river, in neat numbered squares of one hundred and sixty acres each. It brought settlers, who took their patches of land on the humps of the hills and in the hollows of the vales. But it did not bring the road.

The Cape Scott district, recently depopulated by the trek to the San Josef Valley and to Holberg, was thus refilled by a new wave of home-seekers. Surveyor H. H. Browne stated in his report for 1912 that while the population from Holberg to Cape Scott had stood at only sixty in 1909, it had risen during the intervening years to an estimated 600, living on a total of 300 pre-emptions. By 1913, the surveyor, still actively engaged in laying out new homesites, found that Cape Scott alone had a population of approximately 200, and that the entire district held about 1000.

The newcomers much resembled their predecessors in their enthusiasm, co-operation, and energy — so much so that there was no perceptible break in the pulse of the settlement in general. About the only difference lay in the fact that, whereas the original hundred persons had been entirely of Danish extraction, the thousand who arrived by the year 1914 represented almost every European nationality. Whereas, in the 1890's, British Columbia had opened its doors to colonists of other than British nationality because not enough Britons were emigrating to Canada to build a population in the Dominion, fifteen years after establishment of the Danish colony at

Cape Scott, a steady flow of land-seekers had filled both unclaimed and abandoned plots of land there with new arrivals from the British Isles. By 1913, a roll call of Township 43 pre-emptors included such names as John Thomas, John A. Jones, Howard F. Drake, Andrew Beveridge, H. S. King, Andrew E. Kelso, Gordon McQueen, Harry Vincent, William H. Gardiner, George Lovell, Charles Silvester Wadey, Charles J. Wadey, Cecil Thompson, John V. Colton, Ranson F. Warren, Albin Williams, F. H. Ward, Ernest I. Searle, Wilfred Sebastian Gibbs, William Collison, John P. Hume, James A. Vick, Walter D. Burke, and Martin Philip Sheridan. English-speaking immigrants thus constituted a large enough majority to cause that language to become more or less the accepted tongue, even in re-occupied homes where mainly the Danish idiom had been heard.

In 1914, the observant H. H. Browne was able to include in his report a comment that:

> Amongst the pre-emptors in Township 37 are a dozen Germans, who have comfortable homes, and who seem ambitious to improve their land, and appear to congratulate themselves on being in Canada. Their relations with their neighbors are amicable.

Individuals and families of Belgian, Polish, Italian, Swedish, Norwegian, Swiss, and other national stock also appeared at the northern end of Vancouver Island. The sudden admixture resulted in some ironic and some humorous situations. At least one couple of differing nationalities could barely understand each other's spoken word during all their years in the settlement. A naive young school teacher solemnly asked a lady friend of hers whether or not, in the event she were to marry a certain Norwegian gentleman then paying suit to her, she would be able to understand her children. Parents eager to learn the language of the new land sometimes found, to their consternation, that their children were bringing home from school the dialect of east London.

But such instances were merely bits of comedy-relief in the drama of the times. The slim rations of literature, the catalogues, and the newspapers that found their way into the district were almost always printed in English. Social gatherings brought all ethnic groups together, in which circumstances, differences in language and national custom disappeared almost entirely under the onslaught of community enterprise.

As more townships were surveyed, and as more settlers took pre-emptions, additional small concentrations of population developed.

The Cape Scott colonists had made Fisherman's Bay, the steamer landing, their focal point. There they had built a store; near there, they had built their parsonage, with space for meetings and school.

After dispersion of the original colony, the center of population shifted toward Hansen Lagoon. Along the road that extended from the junction with the Holberg trail to the dyke, the new wave of settlers built a church, with solid pews and stained glass windows, a Post Office, and a community hall, which also served as a school. The hall was typical of the projects undertaken by this community. It was built to accommodate, and many times did accommodate, as many as two hundred people at public gatherings. During the peak population years, a second store did business at Fisherman's Bay, and the Vick family home acted as a stopping-place for travellers waiting the indeterminate arrival of whatever passenger-freight boat was on the run from there to Shushartie or Quatsino.

Some ten miles down-island, Henry Ohlsen opened a store on the banks of the San Josef River in 1908, and was made Postmaster that same year. Where the trail from Cape Scott hit the river bank, a hundred yards from his home, Ohlsen built the store, which would also house the Post Office. The building was of sawn lumber, brought, along with other general freight, in small lots up the shallow river. Quite modern in any small community in its day, the building stood two storeys high, with a great false front and large plate glass windows. The second floor held living quarters for his mother.

Here, where travellers had, often, to wait for a skiff to return from across the river, the federal government built a wharf as moorage for one of the skiffs, and as a landing on to which mail and freight could be unloaded from the boats serving the west coast.

One would need to look far and wide in British Columbia today for anything resembling the general store in this farthest-west settlement of 1910 and thereabouts. In addition to grocery essentials, it was required to stock boots and shoes, clothing, tools, kitchen utensils, bedding, lamps and lanterns, candles, kerosene, guns and ammunition, hay and grain, drugs and patent medicines, and, of course, a necessary adjunct to the home, already mentioned in this story — stoves.

It could stock canned meats and bacon, but not fresh meat. Some of the original Cape Scott settlers had brought in cattle. When most of this group dispersed, N. P. Jensen and Theo Fredericksen continued to raise beef and dairy herds. Alfred Spencer, who arrived at the Lagoon meadowlands with the later wave of pre-emptors, also took to raising cattle, chiefly for beef. Most settlers either relied on deer from the forest and trout from the lakes and streams or else went without fresh meat and fish.

Even though Henry Ohlsen, at San Josef Bay, served the needs of probably three hundred settlers, during the peak population years, he saw most of his customers mainly at boat time. The typical settler had to depend on what he could earn during his stints of fishing or logging "outside" to tide him — and, for some, his family — over the months spent on his pre-emption. His earnings he kept in a roll — perhaps tucked into a sock, the poor man's wallet. Since he must spend six months of each year "proving up" his claim, he could not make continued trips away from home to recompense for careless spending. As earnings from seasonal jobs were generally meagre, what money there was had to be budgeted severely to make it stretch to the next earning period.

A search made by the Department of Lands for this story indicated that ninety-three pre-emptions were claimed in the San Josef Bay and lower San Josef Valley area. Not many of these homesites could be seen from the river; but, for some years, a visitor making his way by small boat up the four or so miles of waterway navigable at high tide saw occupied dwellings along both banks.

Erik Petersen's cabin, crowded against the base of a low mountain, and raised above high tides and freshets on huge logs of spruce, guarded the southern entrance. Eugene Falck, around the beginning of World War I, would build just above the sand beach, on the northern shore. Farther up the south bank, the Green and Clarkson families took adjoining pre-emptions, cleared land, and planted large vegetable gardens and berry patches. Axel Andersen built his cabin at the river's first bend, and Charles Dickens lived in solitude only a short distance up-river from Henry Ohlsen, on the opposite shore. Just above Dickens, Arthur Owen Jones built quite a "modern" home for his family at the water's edge. Past the main bend of the river, Cecil Ashby found flat land for garden and orchard, and for beds of flowers, his enduring passion.

As the main trail did not give access to the river above Henry Ohlsen's home, not many land-seekers chose to build near its bank on this side. Henry's mother took a claim up-stream from his pre-emption. Her property rounded the main bend, where the aboriginal village of Nohm had once stood, facing a large pool. Along this pool, Captain Henry Petersen had built a cabin upon his removal from the Cape Scott colony, and before his removal once more to Sea Otter Cove. As far up the river as a skiff could travel, the Andersens, first of the Cape Scott Danes to relocate along the San Josef, had found large natural meadows around which to stake their several properties. Peder Andersen chose as a family homesite a lea ringed with tall spruce and balsam trees. Not long after the house was built, a great gale sprang up. Great trees were blown down, but none touched the house. Jens Hansen — the Andersens' only neighbor — fearing that he would be in danger in his home, rushed outdoors, and was crushed under a giant windfall.

The Shown family took land in South Bay, as the bight inside Cape Palmerston was known, and my mother pre-empted a strip of land left over from the square plots laid out by the surveys — a wedge-shaped parcel, two miles or so toward Sea Otter Cove from the river mouth, facing a mile of sand beach.

With store and Post Office, and with at least a rudimentary land and water transportation system, the imagination could visualize at San Josef Bay the beginnings of a prosperous, permanent community. The practical eye, however, saw the settlement's tenuous position. It was almost as if the place were some sort of mysterious Shangri-La, the inhabitants of which wished to keep its location secret from the rest of the world.

By land, it was connected to both Holberg and Fisherman's Bay by mile after mile of single-file trail in either direction. By water, its only entry involved, at maximum spring tide, crossing a submerged sand-bar, threading two pillar-like rocks at the river's mouth, and, for any but the shallowest of craft, bumping over a series of ancient sunken logs. To Henry Ohlsen, San Josef was indeed a sort of Shangri-La. He lived there forty years, and died there, well beyond man's allotted three score and ten.

Lake Erie, during the years of peak population, became the district's busiest crossroad — that is, cross-trail. Where the trail from San Josef Bay touched the lake, a trail to the left led down into Sea Otter Cove. A small pier served travellers who might wish to row across the lake, or to any spot on its shores. To the right, another trail led to the community hall.

The hall at Cape Scott at least had the advantage of a roadside location, to which lumber could be hauled by horse-drawn vehicle. In addition, it stood in the midst of a comparatively densely populated area. The Lake Erie Hall site was three miles, most of this distance up-hill, from the nearest harbor. The spot was surrounded, not by a community, but by unbroken forest.

Pre-emptions, however, lay in all directions from this point — it formed a centre, even though only a mathematical centre, by the intersection of diameters from the shoreline of San Josef Bay to Lake William and from practicable walking distance either way along the Cape Scott-Holberg trail.

In a decision typical of the settlers of that district, convenience in reaching the hall was put above convenience in its construction. The site chosen fronted Lake Erie, presenting a most favorable view of that beautiful piece of water. Walls and roof were constructed from materials at hand, but only the best fir flooring went under the dancers' feet. Anonymous pre-emptors, not all of whom cared to dance themselves, carried the lumber up the three-mile grade on their backs, and built the hall with no funds but their own.

Beyond the hall, the trail crossed the stream that flowed from Lake Erie, and plunged north-east, beneath high hemlock and balsam growth, toward Lake William. Along the trail, the Tenant family and Ben Luding found natural meadows in which to build and, on the lake, Jack Wilder made a clearing and built a cabin on the south-west shore. On the banks of the natural canal joining Lake William and Lake Brink, Peter Obling, one of the settlement's most isolated pre-emptors, made his home on a spot the beauty of which, to the young immigrant, overrode its inconvenient location. George Hilroy took land and built near the upper end of Lake Brink, about two miles from my father's claim.

There were others around these two lakes — I saw their clearings and their abandoned homes years later, when I spent a winter in Ben Luding's cabin — but I never thought to ask the handful of survivors about all of those who had long gone. Always, as my partner, Roland Spencer, and I walked this part of our trapline, or, more interested in looking for signs of humanity than of mink or marten, paddled the lakes in dug-outs left at shore, we talked and pondered about the vanished people. But we never could penetrate the air of mystery that hung over the calm water, the quiet woods, the futile little clearings, and the vacant cabins. Perhaps, if learning an answer could accomplish nothing, it is better that the mystery remained unsolved.

The trail to Sea Otter Cove, from the San Josef end of Lake Erie, passed through the pre-emption of Jack Rayfield and wandered westward toward the shore. Here, the ground fell away to skirt a terrain so swampy that more direct access to San Josef Bay was literally cut off. Even so, when, fifteen years after the last settler had gone, my grand-uncle, Henry Ohlsen, in giving instructions on how to find and follow this trail, added as a word of caution, "Whenever possible, stick to the down logs; don't step off!" My partner and I did manage to find the trail, and it did consist mainly of felled trees.

The harbor was covered from shore to shore with Canada geese. Some flocks of these birds fly no farther south than this in their winter migration. Food is abundant here, and at sea level the temperature seldom falls below freezing. Hardly a sign remained of the once-busy settlement.

Although he knew the anchorage to be unsafe, Captain Henry Petersen, year after year, moored the *Cape Scott* here, in a haven relatively safer than any other north of Winter Harbor.

Most of Sea Otter Cove's pre-emptors were bachelors. Carter, Harestad, Simmonsen, Donesetti, Carlson, Nozzler, Caruso, and others built along the harbor's shores. Beyond the harbor, toward Hansen Lagoon, John Laurie built his home and grew prolific flowers and vegetables just above the beach named after Captain Henry Lowrie. The Rasmussen family, along with Captain Petersen's younger daughter, Nora, gave Sea Otter Cove entitlement to a public school for a very few years. Both Rasmussen and Petersen, after having spent years of their lives in an attempt to bring success to the Cape Scott colony, tried for years to make a settlement at Sea Otter Cove.

With a Post Office in the Rasmussen home, and a community hall and school, this small isolated bay, for a time, lived as a more compact population centre than any other of the many tiny localities that made up the "North End". One of the first places, beyond the Lagoon vicinity, to be settled, it became also one of the first deserted. When I saw it, in mid-winter of 1936, only Julius Rasmussen visited the cove regularly, during monthly calls at San Josef Bay. Usually in January, when pelts were at their best, Julius would spend a few weeks near his former home, taking what he had found to be the number of mink he could allot himself on a sustained yield basis. As he lived aboard his boat during such trips, he left no mark ashore. While Julius was absent, the closely-woven forest about the shores looked as if its cool green tapestry had never been broken; and the waters of the cove itself seemed never to have felt the presence of anything more than its timeless flocks of migratory geese.

As settlers moved from all sides towards the center, a trail was gradually completed along the eastern edge of Lake Erie, and on from there in a more or less direct line for Holberg, cutting into the old San Josef Valley trail not far from the Andersen meadows. This main east-west trail crossed the old route from San Josef Bay to Lake William at the base of a hemlock not far from the Lake Erie community hall. Someone possessed of an historic language sense dubbed this crossroads marker the Witness Tree. Signs nailed to its trunk pointed for wayfarers the destination of each trail's end. Posters, notices, and scraps of witticism gradually accumulated about this guidepost, some to remain until long after all for whom the messages were intended had gone.

The Witness Tree filled my imagination with ghosts more than could the sight of any depopulated home. Here it was that the throng of silent, booted, packboard-bearing pioneers had trod by, north, south, east and west, as the mute signs guided them. Many times I paused in its silent setting, to rest, and to look for a mark of some footprint other than my own. When I passed it for the last time, it pointed for me, as it had already done for so many others, the way out.

Halfway up Lake Erie, Charley Verner's cabin formed the lower boundary of another compact cluster of homes. Here, for a mile or so, steep hillsides rose on either side of the lake's upper end. On patches of level ground near where St. Mary's Creek flowed near the lake, and farther along, where the stream wound through natural meadow, "Old" MacDonald, Fred Larsen, the Hopkins family, Martin Olafsen, the Nygrens, and Bullock took land and built homes or cabins near adjacent boundaries.

During the settlement's comparatively prosperous years, a visitor would have found the Lake Erie locale a most idyllic setting. Never ruffled by winds, the lake stretched like a mirror through its mile and a half of length. Settlers could visit neighbors by rowing or paddling from shore to shore if they preferred water to land travel. The main trail followed the eastern shore just above the waterline, giving a traveller on foot a constantly changing view as the peaceful strip of water reflected wooded hills rising above both banks of the lake for its full length.

I saw the lake, from both on it and beside it. In summer, a drenching shower could be followed by such a clear, sunny day that the rain was soon forgotten. In winter, year after year, a flock of swans made this spot home, their startling white forms silhouetted sharply against the lake's hemlock-green surface. Sometimes, moving soundlessly along in an abandoned skiff or dug-out canoe, I used to think of Carl Olson, first pioneer to build on these shores. I imagined him, as I had seen him in an old tin-type photograph, rowing on the lake, his dog standing at the boat's stern; and I could visualize why he, and others after him, had come to live with the tranquility and the beauty of Lake Erie.

The trail north-west to the junction with the Lagoon road ran through a country that varied from a forest of yellow cedar to scrub "Nebraska" country. A few settlers made their homes here, but this world, made strange by the wandering Fisherman River, soon drove them to move on. Beaver dams had so changed the river's channels that a walker attempting to follow its course found himself in an unending nightmare of cul de sacs, in vegetation so dense that passageway had to be cut, step by step, mile after mile.

The Fredericksens came more than five miles to pick wild cranberries here for sauce to garnish their Christmas goose. As to native peoples who, far into the past, had lived from what Nature offered, it was a good land to the young Fredericksens, themselves born to a land sometimes, and in some places, forbidding to those unfamiliar with it.

Some other settlers did adopt the new land as their life-long home. Captain Petersen remained there to the end, as did Henry Ohlsen and his mother, Jack Rayfield, N. P. Jensen, Charley Verner, Knute Hansen, and a few others — but not many. Most came away, sooner or later. Some, although they were to leave the settlement, adopted it sincerely while they stayed, and pondered on its appearance, its character, and its mystery.

One of these self-schooled philosophers was Bertel Christian Bekker, who took land in 1899 midway between Hansen Lagoon and Fisherman's Bay, astride the old trail that followed the meadow stream. He remained there for some twenty years, until he could hardly be blamed for having followed others out again. In 1919, Bekker wrote the following reminiscent sketch of his new homeland for the Victoria *Colonist:*

I thought it a well known fact that the British Empire consisted of Cape Scott and a good many larger and smaller countries scattered all over the world. As a proof that this definition holds good, I can point to any Canadian geography. The authors of these useful books have obviously considered the aforesaid definition an axiom, and consequently have not found it worth while mentioning.

A line drawn across the Island from Parksville to Alberni is about as far as the good old Colonist goes — all that is known of this most important part of the Empire. The people in general, and the Development League in particular, do not seem to care for the fact that the end is not yet.

CONSIDERABLE TERRITORY

There is a vast country, by no means unpopulated, on the very north end of this beautiful Island — a country rich in excellent farm land, lakes, rivulets and brooks. Full of fish, big marshes, tide flats, and meadows. To this day in undisputed possession of elk, deer, bear, wolf, beaver and, in Summertime, the willow grouse. In Winter, the marshes, meadows and flats are the haunts of countless numbers of waterfowl.

It is this country I would like to describe to the public, and the Development League may find it worth while being acquainted with it.

The north end of this Island is not mountainous; it is hilly. The hills are gravelly; in some places will be found black limestone or a white clayish matter called soapstone. The low land is black, subsoil blue sand, in many places with traces of placer gold. Depth of soil from two to four feet, sometimes much deeper. The growth on the hills is hemlock, cedar, cypress and an occasional blue pine. The underbrush is salal and huckleberry. The same trees are found on the low lands, together with balsam and spruce. On the so-called bottom-land, old river or sea bottom, heavy spruce are scattered far apart from one another, and in between is a dense growth of salmon berry or wild black currant. On former tide flats will be found crab apples or alder, with fine grass in between.

We will now take a walk from Cape Scott, the west corner of the north end, to Shushartie Bay, the east corner.

NATURAL CURIOSITIES

About thirteen years ago I, together with a friend and his dog, took a trip around the Cape. We went forth in spite of the old saying that when two or more encircle the Cape, one will be missing when the starting-point is reached. There are many natural freaks to be seen. First is "The Well". This is a hole about four feet in diameter straight down in solid rock. How deep it is is not known; but about twenty feet down is water. It would be a waste of time to try to pump this water out. The well is supplied from unknown subterranean channels extending out into the ocean.

Next is "The Stump", a gigantic piece of rock cast of the same material as the Cape — a piece of clever sculpture made by Mother Nature herself.

Then comes "The Cave". How deep this cave goes in is not known. It has never been explored. Probably it extends to the very core of the old Cape. People have tried to get in, but as soon as they lose sight of the light through the entrance, they lose their courage too, and hike back as fast as they can.

Sometimes supernatural groaning and rumbling sounds are heard from the interior. "It is water," say the Whites; they always want to trace things back to natural causes. But the Indians know better. "It is the ghost," they say; and whenever they hear the sound they take their headgear off in salutation, fear and awe, standing up in their frail crafts, keeping one eye on the Cape, another on the sea, where sea lions are bobbing up from the depths, standing in rows like soldiers at attention, fury in their eyes, glittering teeth, and water trickling down their dark, smooth hides. Everything is imposing and awe-inspiring here.

Scott Channel, as the water is called here, between Cape Scott and Scott Island — about two miles out — has a very threatening aspect. Like foam-bedecked roaring monsters, the green waves are advancing, with untiring perseverence, trying to overthrow the old Cape, only to be smashed against the flint-hard rock. A tremendous waste of power. Not a wrinkle is smoothed; not an edge or projection blunted in the rock. The Cape is as unimpressed as the day it shot up from the bowels of old Mother Earth.

After the cave comes "The Breathing Hole". This is a hole about six inches in diameter. "The Cape is breathing through that," says the Indian. "It is suction," says the prosaic White man. Hold your hand over it and feel the exhalation. When the sea is rough, insert a pole; the exhalation will throw it high up in the air, followed by a spout of water.

A LEGEND

Once upon a time, a fishing vessel anchored off the Cape and sent a boat to shore in search of fresh water. The men got the water, and also nuggets as large as acorns. The beach was strewn with them, was the report. The vessel went to Victoria with a cargo of fish and many nuggets. Afterwards, the ship went back for further investigation, but was lost with all hands on board. Since then, nobody could recover the spot where the gold had been found. "An extraordinary low tide," explains the White man. "The spirit of the Cape took it and hid it in the woods," says the Indian, and he is probably right. There surely is a nugget under each tree and tiny root on the north end of Vancouver Island! Remove them and the nuggets will grow, and the more you dig the better they grow, transformed into waving golden grain-fields.

This is Cape Scott, admired by the Whites, feared by the Indians, loved by the few who know.

The starting-point is reached — but the dog is missing. "Lost in one of the many nooks," says my friend. He came back, though, a day later, looking as if he had had a narrow escape of some kind.

ONCE AN ISLAND

In pre-historic times, Cape Scott was separated from the Island by a short, narrow channel. The never-resting surf has filled this channel. Where it was is now about two acres of land, consisting of low sandhills covered with grass and flowers. This is called "The Sandneck". These peaceful, flower-bedecked hills have a notorious reputation in the history of the Indians. The Sandneck is an old native camping ground. Heaps of burned shells from mussels, mixed with bones, broken kitchen utensils, and other Indian odds and ends are found here. Mussels grow here wherever water can reach. Many of them contain pearls, but too small to be of value.

INDIAN BATTLES

Many a royal battle between Cape Scott and Quatsino Indians has been fought here, as human bones still found here bear witness. As far as the Indians are concerned, the Sandneck is a haunted place. The tale goes that close to a hundred years ago, the Indians from Quatsino made a raid on the Cape Scott Indians, with the result that the latter were almost exterminated, the only survivor being a woman with a boy of four. They managed to escape in a canoe. About fifteen years ago, the author knew this boy, then a very old man, known as "Old Chief George". His real name was "Keketi". I can see him yet, a small, light-built man, cap cocked on one ear; small, dark, sparkling eyes, and a tremendous hooked eagle beak of a nose, the latter not common among Vancouver Island Indians. Keketi as a boy of four went to the Mainland. There he grew up, became chief of another tribe, and returned to the Sandneck. Then came another evil day, when he and his followers collided with the Whites. They were then taught a lesson that made the West Coast Indians submissive to the Whites from then on.

AN INTERESTING TALE

Here is the tale as it was told by the camp-fire in an old deserted shanty. In the early part of the 'eighties, word came to Victoria to the effect that the Indians camped on the Sandneck at Cape Scott had murdered a White prospector. A gunboat departed to investigate, eventually capture and bring to justice the perpetrator. Upon arriving off the Sandneck, a boat was sent ashore, demanding the deliverance of the murderer. After some "pow-wow", it was refused and the boat compelled to leave, hooted and jeered at by the infuriated savages. Three shells were then fired from the ship. One was blank; another fell short; and the third went home with such effect that the redskins never forgot it. The next boat ashore took the murderer on board the ship, and a few minutes later, he was seen hanging from the mast. The body was afterwards taken ashore and left to the terror-stricken friends. After this, the Sandneck was *deserted for many years, elk and deer being in sole possession of the green sandhills.*

DEEP BAY SETTLEMENT

Half an hour's walk will take us from Cape Scott to Deep Bay. From there, a short road leads to the Lagoon. The Lagoon is a stretch of mud-flats; the upper end is grassland. In 1902 and 1903, nine of the settlers dyked this grassland and divided it among themselves, each taking ten acres. This soil is black and very rich, subsoil blue sand, with traces of gold. The dyke is 1,100 feet long, bottom width twenty feet, three feet on tip, and seven feet high. There is a sluice gate, with four gates and a sluice box. The material is taken from the spot. A ditch fourteen feet wide and three feet deep was dug on each side, the dirt thrown and wheeled up thus forming the dyke. The turf was carefully cut into square pieces and piled, forming a protective coat over the interior. Afterwards it was fenced on both sides and a gravel path made on top. Summer tides never flood the entire mud flats; consequently, never reach the dyke. From the dyke to the inlet of the flats, called Goose Harbor, is about two miles. The inlet is 300 feet wide. At low tide, the water depth is only a few inches. The highest tide is here fifteen feet, and at the dyke, six feet. The Lagoon is Cape Scott's sporting place.

NATURE'S VARIED MOODS

In summer, the Lagoon is the scene of great activity. Cow bells are ringing, and vehicles are travelling the good, broad road the Government has built through the grasslands to the dyke. Mowers and scythes are busy and, in the latter part of August, hundreds of haycocks are seen. The air is dense with the smell of cured hay; meadow lark and robin voice contention in rippling notes; and the pygmy owl is busy hunting grass-hoppers. It is a wonderful, smiling spot, surrounded by morose and silent forests.

But see the same Lagoon in Fall and Winter! Then the ditches grow to creeks, and the creeks into roaring rivers. Everywhere are sounds of water in motion, and in the air is a wheezing, seething mass of flapping bird wings.

SPORTMAN'S PARADISE

This is the chance for the hunter. Shots are fired everywhere, making the air so full of holes that it is a marvel one can breathe. Teal, mallard, spoonbill, butterball, pintail and merganser — this is the selection; and from Christmas on, the big honker and kackling are thrown in for good measure. The trumpeter swan has chosen the marshes in the woods. It is a grand time! Never mind the water; it is not deep and, owing to absence of snow and mountains, not cold. Some people even say it is not wet, but that may be called an illusion.

A drawback to Cape Scott is the absence of a suitable harbor for big vessels. Fisherman's Bay is the best, but it is open and exposed to northern winds. If a breakwater were built, and material is available on the spot, there could be a good harbor. At the present time there is connection by motor schooner, the Cape Scott II, Captain Henry Petersen, from Quatsino village, where the S.S. Maquinna calls, to Fisherman's Bay. Sometimes, also, big steamers from Vancouver call at the Bay, and landing is effected by small boats.

The coast from Cape Scott to Shushartie Bay, about thirty miles, is a continuous row of sand beaches, broken by projecting rocky points. Cape Scott beach, one and a half miles long; Deep Bay beach, two miles; Sunset beach, two miles; the long beach, four miles; and the beach from Cape Commerel [Sutil] to Shingle Point, close to Shushartie Bay, supposed to be eight miles long.

SETTLEMENTS ABOUND

There are settlements along the whole coast. The beaches are broad and the sand so hard and smooth that they can offer most splendid sporting and race grounds for bicycles and autos. Good landings for aeroplanes can probably be found, too.

When the Island Highway is extended to these shores, the old Cape, with its freaks and nooks, would be the Island's greatest attraction. Gay laughter would echo under its wig of old, knotty, storm-beaten trees. Children would play hide-and-go-seek on the hills of the Sandneck. Autos would be racing to and fro, and golf and foot balls would be bouncing on the broad beaches.

And then, when the season is over and the tourists home, tales and adventures would be told, and it would be admitted that there is a North End attached to this beautiful Island of ours, and a very interesting and good one at that.

Bekker, writing in 1919, while settlers were leaving on every outgoing vessel, could foresee the day when the Cape Scott settlement would revert to nature. Whether through imagination or vision, he also foresaw a renewed interest in his favorite forest trails and sandy beaches. However, a reader soon discovers that Bekker, the naturalist, would have opposed progress which might alter or despoil the elemental qualities of his strange new land.

THE EAST COAST

As has been mentioned before in this account, the area which became generally known as "Cape Scott" or "The North End" stretched down the east coast of Vancouver Island to Shushartie Bay, a distance of about thirty miles.

In aboriginal times, life in this section of coast centered at Nahwitti village, located at Cape Sutil. When the first Europeans arrived, this chief village gave its name to a numerous and powerful sept of the Kwakiutls located in lesser villages all the way from Shushartie Bay north to Cox Island.

While traders and explorers never did meet many natives along the west coast north of Quatsino Sound, here, upon the eastern shores of the Island, they came upon Indians all along the coast, with a mighty "capital" at Nahwitti.

The coming of Europeans brought nothing but tragedy to the Nahwittis.

In 1786, James Stuart Strange found the native people quite friendly, and willing to barter. In 1792, Captain George Vancouver was well received by Chief Cheslakee at his village on the Nimpkish River. Don Galiano, in that same year, left many trade beads as gifts with the Nahwitti people, at their Cape Sutil chief village.

During the next twenty years, as the number of trading vessels increased, and the number of sea-otter pelts decreased, relationships between native Indians and White traders disintegrated.

In 1811, prompted, perhaps, by injustices suffered at the hands of some previous trader, natives of, it is believed, Nahwitti village, surprised and killed the crew of the Astor America Fur Company's *Tonquin*. On going below, the Nahwittis accidentally detonated the ship's magazine, destroying the vessel and themselves in the process.

Twice within the space of one year, the village was destroyed by naval gunfire; by HMS *Daedalus* in 1850, and by HMS *Daphne* in 1851. Both attacks were ordered by Richard Blanshard, first Governor of the Crown Colony of Vancouver Island, in retaliation for the deaths of several seamen. It would appear that natives of this village were not clearly known to have caused the deaths for which they paid most dearly.

The Nahwitti people apparently rebuilt their village on the same site, for it appears as an Indian village in the 1864 *Vancouver Pilot*.

When Dr. J. W. Powell, Indian Superintendent for British Columbia, visited the Nahwitti people in 1879, they had removed to Mel-oopa, on the south-west shore of Hope Island. They had done so, they said, because of a greatly reduced population.

Some, but not many natives still occupied this village on Hope Island when the north end settlers built homes along the Vancouver Island shore, near the site of the former Nahwitti chief village, early in the twentieth century. Dr. Powell reported that many Mel-oopa villagers met violent deaths, presumably through either turmoil within the village or raids from outside, resulting from the liquor trade. The village finally became completely deserted — in the 1920's, it would seem, from the presence of calendars in homes. As late as 1960, skeletons in coffins still occupied some of the deserted buildings. Gunshot holes in skulls remained as testimony to the manner in which some of these last Mel-oopa inhabitants had died. Surviving Nahwittis travelled south to Alert Bay, leaving only their name to the once-populous homeland.

This north-eastern coast of Vancouver Island, from Shushartie up-coast to Cape Scott, developed a settlement pattern considerably different from that established at Cape Scott. The main difference would appear to have stemmed from the fact that, whereas the first settlers made their way to Cape Scott by means of an organized colonization effort, the first east coast land-seekers arrived individually.

In 1883, Robert Hunt was allowed to purchase a block of about 160 acres along the eastern shore of Shushartie Bay, in accordance with the Land Act of 1882. This Act permitted a bona fide settler to stake a claim of land before it was surveyed. In some communities, such as Gibson's Landing, where George Gibson staked a claim in 1886, under the same Land Act, subsequent surveys coincided with the original land claim. The first Cape Scott settlers did not have definite land boundaries until after Ernest Cleveland's surveys of their proposed properties were complete. At Shushartie, the original Lot 5, claimed by Hunt, did not fit into the rectangular pattern established a decade later.

In 1891, James Helmcken, son of Dr. J. S. Helmcken, purchased a lot at the head of Shushartie Bay. William McGary claimed the entire western shore and built a home and trading post near the head of the bay.

By 1893, when Government Surveyor H. M. Burwell was assigned to add to existing surveys from Shushartie to Cape Scott, he was able to take passage on the steamer *Coquitlam* from Vancouver. From Shushartie, however, he took to a dug-out canoe to make his way up the treacherous coastline. Another steamer, the SS *Boscowitz,* took the surveyor south again from Shushartie at the end of November that year.

With the discovery of gold in the Yukon in 1897, coastal shipping increased phenomenally. Skippers heading north out of Vancouver found that ports-of-call such as Shushartie were quite conveniently on course.

In 1913, a fish cannery was built in Shushartie Bay by the Goletas Fish Company, with William Lord as manager. This industry, added to the fact that steamer traffic — first by Canadian Pacific, and later, by Union Steamships Company — ended here, made Shushartie a comparatively busy harbor for some years.

What was known for many years as Shushartie consisted of the establishment begun by Jephtha Skinner — a home building that functioned as an inn — to accompany his own passenger and freight service. After his death by drowning, his family continued to operate the home facilities as a steamer port-of-call.

Even after the cannery ceased to operate, after a few years, and the collapse of settlements to the north dried up the flow of passengers and freight, Shushartie remained a regular stop for up-coast Union Steamships vessels. The *Venture,* capable of but eight knots, at cruising speed, kept the port open throughout the depression years of the 1930's. Then, as the Cape Scott settlements had survived the pre-1914 depression, only to be destroyed by the Great War and its aftermath; so was Shushartie by World War II and its aftermath.

Ten miles up-island from Shushartie Bay, the Nahwitti River flows into Queen Charlotte Sound. Sand from its waters has, over the years, created a shallow bar which almost encircles Hope Island, to the south-east. On the shores of a lagoon at the river's mouth, a meeting place for Indians of Queen Charlotte Sound had existed from time immemorial. Especially during summer months, this place became the center for the native people's halibut fishery. Using a special hook, with an elongated barb, the Indians filled their canoes with fish from the sandy floor of the Nahwitti Bar. Ashore, they cut the fish into strips to sun-dry for a staple winter food.

In the year 1910, Frank Bragg was in charge of dining room stores for the Canadian Pacific Railway in Vancouver, British Columbia. Year after year, he had watched both Canadian Pacific trains and ships leave the port terminus for far-away places, with a growing feeling that life was passing him by. In the British Columbia Government's offer of free land at the northern end of Vancouver Island, he saw an opportunity to gain a degree of freedom and independence never to be gained from his job.

Robert Bromley and George Lycett, who worked with Bragg, and who shared his revolt against the restrictions of their occupation, joined him in his plan to trek north.

So, in the summer of 1910, the three men and their families booked passage on the Union Steamship *Vadso*. When they reached their destination, they were lightered ashore by the steamer's lifeboat. On a site selected just above the beach, at the mouth of the Nahwitti, the men built cabins for their families on mutual ground and close together.

Behind the cabins, burial boxes stuck among the limbs of spruce trees comprised the sole evidence of the busy native village that had once occupied this same spot.

One settler, by the name of Samson, had, years before, built a cabin at this same place, and had filled it with books. At the first sign of company, the recluse had fled, presumably to a location still more remote.

Henry Darlington, who had known the Braggs in Vancouver, made his way north to join the settlement and to marry the elder Bragg daughter. His brother, Archie, built a cabin nearby. So did Jack Wilson and his inseparable companion, Jack Hardy. Albert Hole and his family, and a MacLean and an Eagen family joined the settlement at the beach, giving it the appearance of a tiny village.

In order to comply with residence regulations, the men had to build shacks on their pre-emptions up the Nahwitti Valley. Between days spent in these minimal quarters and days spent "outside" to earn needed cash, they had none too much time with their families; but they agreed that to build homes scattered at half-mile intervals through the thick forest would have worked too great a hardship on wives and children. Moreover, a compact gathering of population at the beach could, in time, qualify for provision of a school and other facilities.

Single pre-emptors who made their way to this part of the island built permanent cabins on their claims up the valley. Stanislaw Tyllia, formerly a Prussian officer, was one of the first to make his home there, on an isolated quarter-section of land. When Ivor Lewis and Sam Hellings, partners, also built cabins up the valley, the Nahwitti showed signs of promising development.

Nahwitti settlers found, for a few years, that there was some employment to be had in the vicinity of their homesites. While detailed surveys, based on transits run by Government Surveyors E. B. Hermon and A. H. Hawkins, in 1891 and 1892, and by H. M. Burwell, in 1893, were being completed, some local settlers could find work as pole men, axe men, packers, and cooks on parties established annually to carry out this work. Surveyors in charge of these parties were also encouraged to purchase produce from local settlers.

The British Columbia Provincial Government, as it had earlier agreed to build a road from Fisherman's Bay to Holberg, now decided to make a start on a road from Nahwitti to Fisherman's Bay. While Shushartie offered the better harbor by far, complete with wharf, rugged terrain between there and Nahwitti prohibited road construction with the elementary facilities available to northern settlers.

Fred Clulow, who had taken a pre-emption on Nigei Island, acted as foreman for work done on the proposed road from Nahwitti. Since many pre-emptors, scattered along miles of coastline, looked to the few dollars that might be earned from such Government work to purchase necessities that could not be made, grown or hunted, large gangs of men could not be congregated at any one spot for this work. Consequently, the road was tackled in pieces along its surveyed route, and each piece extended until, hopefully, it joined some other similarly constructed piece.

My father saw the Bragg family at their Nahwitti home during the summer following their arrival. They spoke enthusiastically of the prospects of their new venture, so my father reminisced for me years later; particularly of the road that was to link their east-coast settlements with the older communities at Fisherman's Bay. My father, who was just then claiming his quarter-section south of Lake Brink, and who had spent two days making his way down the bewildering Nahwitti Valley, also expressed his optimism for the anticipated road.

Within the next two years, a section of road extending from Gold Beach, to the south of Nahwitti, to a point somewhat north of Cache Creek was more or less completed, but the advent of World War I hopelessly deferred continuation to Fisherman's Bay.

It is easy now for an analyst to comment, within the vision of retrospect, on the reasons why the construction of a road through this remote part of the province could not succeed, and to conclude that the land-seeker of the time who believed in its success was only dreaming. Yet, in 1911, the same year that construction was started on this portion of the northern Vancouver Island roads, far to the south, another road was being built. It inched along the mainland shore of the province, from Gibson's Landing, on the western entrance to Howe Sound, to Sechelt, fifteen miles farther upcoast. Photographs taken along sections of this route a year after completion show patches of grass growing, unmolested by traffic.

Even ten years later, literally no one as yet walked the full length of this road, scarcely a horse and buggy made its way from end to end, and the very rare automobile driver who attempted a return trip found some hills so rough that they were almost impassable even during the best of weather conditions. At this same time — during the 1920's — a driver endeavoring to make his way from New Westminster to Langley, along the then Yale Road, later to be known as the Trans Canada Highway, faced the possibility, during winter months, of having all four tires torn from his wheels by the sides of frozen ruts.

These latter roads persisted, and were gradually improved. By 1911, a network of many miles of road had already developed in the community of Gibson's Landing, although its population hardly exceeded that of the Nahwitti-Fisherman's Bay district, and although construction conditions were probably comparable. The existence of roads such as these on the lower mainland made possible an economy and a population that without them could not have evolved. Had either the road to Holberg or the road to Shushartie from Fisherman's Bay been completed and maintained, a population quite wholesome to the province's economic health might have remained solidly rooted at the northern end of Vancouver Island. Without either road, continued existence of any sort of practicable settlement became impossible.

A mile inland, and a mile toward Cape Scott from Nahwitti, settlers came upon a lake slightly more than a half mile in length. It so caught the fancy of the Olson brothers, Karl and Pete Shurick and their families, and other pre-emptors that they named it Lake Beautiful. Hydrographic Survey charts now list it as Heimra Lake.

Someone dubbed the stream draining this lake into Shuttleworth Bight Irony Creek, and the name has been retained on charts. The Stranby River, or Cache Creek, as halibuters named it, from the fact that boats cached goods ashore there, was the scene of a minor "rush" during the years that prospectors were examining literally every inch of British Columbia's coastline for gold. Gold was found both in the stream and in black sands on the beach. The black sand, however, also yielded iron pyrites: "fool's gold". The name "Irony" Creek thus symbolizes, no doubt, some story of hopes dashed to earth. Zinc deposits were found along this stream, but they proved of no value to the settlers.

When the Danish colonists travelled past the mouth of Cache Creek in the spring of 1897, a lone Dane, Soren Christiansen, had already lived there for three years. His name is commemorated by Soren Hill, a low knob that rises from the flat terrain behind the bay. A large piece of the shoreline was purchased by a land development company and subdivided into plots. These homesites were occupied and abandoned again within a short span of time.

One settler who did not leave was Harry Shuttleworth, who built a home for his family on a point of land near the river mouth toward Cape Scott. By 1913, the tiny community had enough children for a one-room school to be opened. A photo of this school population, kept by one of the students, Annie Shuttleworth — later Daines — shows the class posed atop a very rough, uncleared bank. As with the population in general, the school failed during the First World War.

So we arrive back at Fisherman's Bay, the anchorage where the first Danish settlers made their way ashore from 1896 to 1900, and where some of the succeeding newcomers continued to land, as group colony gave way to individual pre-emption.

In fact, the two phases of settlement, colony and individual pre-emption, overlapped very little in time. Up to about 1909, the original colonists had the territory much to themselves. As has been mentioned here already, a combination of inadequate harbor at Fisherman's Bay, a provincial government decision to halt additional immigration into the colony, and lack of the promised road link to Quatsino Sound forced the colony settlement, as conceived in 1896, to dissolve. What individual pre-emption took place prior to 1909 was carried out mainly by members of the colony as it disbanded.

By 1909, trails radiated from the head of Hansen Lagoon up-island to Cape Scott, down the middle of the island to Sea Otter Cove, San Josef Bay, Raft Cove and Holberg, and down the east coast to Shushartie.

These trails, as described earlier in this story, varying from good to almost impassable, were to prove incapable of sustaining a permanent population. To those hardy enough to make their way to the northern end of Vancouver Island, these narrow, winding footpaths served, for a time at least, to thread communities and individual pre-emptions into some semblance of a unit.

Those who remained long enough to build homes and clear land felt quite positively that the trails would in due course become roads. Meanwhile, they used the trails. To some, such as Cecil Ashby, the trails did constitute a sort of common entity. Ashby wandered them from home to home. In a packsack, he carried seeds and grafted fruit tree shoots. Like the famed Johnny Appleseed of American folk lore, he scattered growing things from his home on the banks of the San Josef River to the end of literally every trail.

Partly through the efforts of Ashby, and partly because pre-emptors needed all the fresh produce they could grow, gardening became popular throughout the northern end of Vancouver Island.

Almost all settlers planted some sort of garden. Ashby himself surrounded his home with not only fruit and vegetable gardens but also with flowers. Throughout the summer, his clearing maintained a glow of varying colors.

Bernt Ronning, nine miles up-island from Holberg, filled acres of his clearing with flowers, shrubs and trees from around the world. Twin monkey-puzzles guarded his gate. Bamboos, rhododendrons, azalias, flowering peaches and oriental maples made themselves as much at home in the garden of the young immigrant from Norway as did chrysanthemums, pansies, delphiniums, asters, phlox, roses and a host of other more common species of the plant world.

Charles Wadey, at Cape Scott, had been a professional gardener in England. To encourage other settlers to grow produce, Wadey inaugurated an agricultural society. By 1914, two years after his arrival in the district, he was able to stage an exhibition in the community hall. About two hundred people attended this rather unusual event. Some exhibitors carried produce over miles of trail, strapped to the indispensable packboard.

Henry Ohlsen, at San Josef Bay, built a cannery. Families who grew more fruit or berries than they could eat fresh carried the surplus to this cannery as partial payment on a grocery bill or to be canned on shares. Taking advantage of the enormous run of creek cohoe that made its way up the San Josef River each fall, Ohlsen also caught and canned what he considered a reasonable take for use during times of the year when fish of any kind were comparatively scarce.

In 1913, the Dominion Government Telegraph Service extended a telephone line from Port Hardy to Coal Harbor, up the West Arm to Holberg, and along the old trail via San Josef Bay to Cape Scott. From Fisherman's Bay, the line was also pushed through toward Shushartie. Apart from a Government branch line to Sea Otter Cove, and a private branch line to the Fredericksen home at the sand neck, very few homes off the main line received telephones. Although costs prohibited much use of this aspect of the service provided, telephone contact could now be made directly as far south as Victoria.

The main advantage offered by the telephone was the linking through conversation of friends separated by miles of difficult trail. There was no true central — the entire system consisted of one sprawling party line. Each user received a call signal consisting of some arrangement of short and long rings. All telephone users heard everyone else's call signals as well as their own.

Henry Ohlsen was assigned one short, one long, one short as his call signal. After the telephone had been installed in his home and tested, Ohlsen received his first call. He reported that, while he had heard the telephone ring, he could hear nothing through the receiver. The linesman returned, all the way from Holberg, and found the line functioning satisfactorily. Only then did Ohlsen discover that his left ear was deaf.

The system was energized through the lifting of a receiver. With normal telephoning, and normal listening, a set of three dry-cell batteries could be expected to last for about a year. Some users, on applying for fresh batteries, complained that theirs had run down, mysteriously, in much less time. Since these same individuals seemed to know a great deal about the private lives of their neighbors, the persistent eavesdroppers were thus soon located.

Individual styles in the vigor and the duration of the ring soon developed and gradually became identified as all telephones were put to use. As the novelty of the instrument wore off, members of a household went about their business. The attuned ear very quickly learned to distinguish who was ringing at the first sound of the bell, and memory of established pattern told for whom the call was intended even before it had been completed.

By 1913 also, a wharf a half mile in length had been built at Holberg. About seven miles of road stretched out towards Fisherman's Bay, where the federal government was contemplating an attempt to construct a breakwater-wharf combination.

These projects and industries lent an air of seeming solidity to the north end settlements. Minor as they were, road and telephone, in particular, seemed to indicate government awareness of this remote part of Canada and, to the settlers, they foreshadowed greater things to come.

CHAPTER V

Undoubtedly, more roads would have been constructed, more wharves built, and more telephone lines strung throughout the district were it not for the outbreak of war in 1914.

Many young men had just made their way across Canada directly from England. The strongest ties being still with their homeland, most of these recent arrivals left their pre-emptions to enlist in the armed services.

For a time, their removal was counter-balanced by slightly older men, some of whom brought families into the communities. After a time, as the war continued, losses were not made up by the arrival of new settlers.

With the country at war, expenditures for public works came to a halt. During the years of this struggle, the settlers were left to their own devices. For a time, the communities survived quite well under this lack of government involvement.

Today, anywhere in British Columbia, the use of such an expression as "Howdy, Stranger!" would seem rather ludicrous. It would not have seemed ludicrous in the north end settlements in 1914. Almost everyone who broke with his old way of life to make his way to this isolated part of Canada before or during World War I did so in order to gain some sort of freedom from an existing frustration. Upon his arrival, he neither wished his own past pried into nor did he pry into the pasts of others. It is not likely that many had anything dark to hide — the wilds are usually too frightening for the evil-doer. It was, rather, a mutual acceptance at face value, with little curiosity as to one another's pedigrees.

The advent of war did little to alter this feeling of inviolate privacy.

When one young immigrant from Britain avowed that he was going to join the army to kill some enemy in retaliation for newspaper accounts of atrocities against Belgian babies, one of his friends said to him, "You have a rifle. Why don't you take it and shoot some of our German neighbors?" Racial tensions during the war remained of such minor significance that not one hostile act resulted. Since all settlers of German origin were landed immigrants, none were interned.

The fact was that, to those who remained in the settlement, the war was something quite remote. They strove to maintain community life in a diminishing population. The agricultural fair at Cape Scott ceased after 1915. Dances in community halls and picnics on sand beaches managed somehow to survive. Some schools closed.

About 1914, Arnold Stackhouse, grandson of the Reverend W. B. Crickmer, well-known missionary at Derby and Yale during the 1858 Gold Rush days, began lay readings around Quatsino Sound area. He was ordained in 1916, and opened a small church at San Josef Bay on St. Joseph's Day, June 20, of that same year.

Henry Ohlsen had held some religious services in his home. Aware of the fact that there was no hope of establishing a Lutheran church, he had turned to the Anglican denomination, which had its up-coast headquarters at Alert Bay. With my father and mother's wedding set for August of 1916, volunteer work on the building was pushed to have it ready for that event, and to provide a room for the itinerant minister during his visits.

The wedding of Emil Peterson and Eva Buol was the only one ever held in the San Josef Church. The waning population simply did not provide any more eligible couples after this time.

The Reverend Stackhouse covered the entire northern end of the Island during his rounds through his very wild parish. In an account written for the Diocesan Gazette, Mr. Stackhouse outlined his final visit, during the summer of 1917. Accompanied by his wife and one son, he landed by steamer at Shushartie, only to find that the regular small mail-boat from there had broken down.

Without passing reference to the fact that he carried an 80-pound pack on this journey, the clergyman reveals a prodigious ability to hike over the north end's varied trails and roads. The family reached the already deserted Nahwitti settlement at noon, found some fresh eggs laid by doomed marooned hens, and had lunch. They reached Cache Creek, a total of sixteen miles, at dusk. There, Mrs. Shuttleworth, who was carrying on with Sunday School work while her husband, Harry, worked "outside" in a munitions plant, put them up for the night.

86

Next day, Stackhouse set out alone over the thirteen miles to Cape Scott, held 11 a.m. service, then continued the twelve-mile hike required to hold evening service in San Josef Church. Next day, he returned for his family, and they made their way, with stops to visit here and there, to Holberg, by trail and road, and thence back to Alert Bay by way of Coal Harbor.

Land surveys continued throughout the early years of the War. In December of 1914, Surveyor H. H. Browne, while alluding to the "present untoward state of affairs", reported that the settlement was in good condition, the population having increased from not much more than 100 to approximately 1000 during the five previous years. Extracts from his report indicate a note of optimism:

There is probably no richer land in British Columbia than the San Josef Valley. It is enormously fertile and it has a climate as equable as the south end of the island . . . There are flower-gardens, too; I saw quite a number of them, and some were at bachelors' houses. Here is a short list of what was observed: Dahlias, daffodils, hyacinths, tulips, chrysanthemums, carnations, hydrangea. Most of these were in profusion. Sweet peas were luxuriant everywhere, and so were pansies, poppies, and nasturtiums. There is a large variety of wild flowers, some of which, I was told, were either rare or unexpected in the locality.

The report also makes note of the fact that a total of 9000 acres had been surveyed throughout the district, and that a pack-trail was being cut along the eastern shores of Lake Erie. In 1914, the communities between Hopkins Landing and Sechelt, referred to previously in this story, although they could not show a population of nearly the north end's 1000, had a grid of probably forty miles of usable road.

A year later, Browne could still report that, so far as his observations went, improvements to pre-emptions were of a lasting character. Some men had done well at fishing; some were working at the Elk Lake Mines, near Quatsino; some had worked on roads and on the land surveys. Altogether, the report concluded, there was a feeling of content among the settlers.

By 1916, however, Government Surveyor L. S. Cokely reported that many pre-emptors, although they had remained in the area long enough to obtain their Crown grants, had abandoned their claims. He attributed the depopulation to lack of roads; but he also indicated that the Government had, of late years, built four-foot trails rather than roads, as an economy measure. Two stores still operated at Cape Scott. Archie Darlington had taken over the old Danish store after

N. C. Nelson had left for Quatsino. Darlington had enlisted at the beginning of the War, and the Vick family now operated this business. They also made rooms in their home available to travellers. At the peak pre-War population, Henry Ohlsen had opened a second general store nearer to the Lagoon. The Dominion Government Telegraph line was being extended down-island to Cache Creek and Shushartie. At Cache Creek, Harry Shuttleworth maintained a store and was also Postmaster of Stranby Post Office there. Mrs. Shuttleworth operated store and Post Office during the War years. Cape Scott, San Josef Bay, Sea Otter Cove and Holberg Post Offices still all remained open.

By 1917, the Dominion Telegraph line had reached Shushartie. Ironically, between there and Cache Creek not one settler remained for it to serve.

While Government surveyors had up to this time retained a positive attitude, in his report of this year, L. S. Cokely pessimistically admitted that many settlers had departed when they could no longer endure the back-breaking effort expended in carrying all goods on their backs along foot-trails. "No stable population will be secured until roads are built . . . " the report continued.

Up to this time, the settlement had survived against all the odds that local conditions could bring against it. It had survived lack of roads. It had survived lack of harbors. It had also survived without the services of a local doctor. It had required no local police officer. It had managed without the payroll of mine or mill.

Now, after having overcome every possible deterrent for twenty years, it was felled by a conflict half way around the world.

By 1917, adult males without dependents were being conscripted. Some north end men avoided participation in the War; others felt obliged to go.

Near Quatsino, the site was being cleared for a pulp mill, to supply war-time demands for cellulose products. The offer of work at this site, to become known as Port Alice, added its indirect force to the direct force of conscription in depopulating the area from Holberg north. Mining activities around Quatsino Sound also intensified as the global conflict continued, absorbing still more men.

The northern end of the island could have become the bread-basket for the fishing, mining and wood-pulp industries of this great inland waterway. Properly exploited, it could have supplied meats, vegetables, fruits, dairy products and eggs in plenty for Quatsino, Jeune Landing, Coal Harbor, Port Alice, and the dozens of mines and logging camps that dotted the Sound.

But the best beef cattle country was located in the burnt-off area east of Fisherman's Bay, and in the natural meadows of what was known as the South Country, between Ronning and the Lower Macjack River. Leafy vegetables and tubers could be grown in prodigious intensity in the humus of Cape Scott and the San Josef Valley. Natural clearings on the hilltops east and south of the Lake William district would have lent themselves, with little effort, to the growing of berries and fruits. The rich grasses of the dyked Lagoon proved, during the years they were grazed, that they could supply milk and butter in amazing quantities, and of amazing richness.

The disheartening element in the story of public works development in the district is the fact that monies were spent, but that they were spent at the wrong times and on wrong priorities. San Josef Bay, Shushartie and Holberg were provided with wharves. The Goodspeed, Fisherman, and Nahwitti Rivers, and many small streams between Cape Scott and Holberg were spanned with bridges and culverts wide enough to accommodate the traffic of a road.

But the crossings were never linked by road. Had even a single main route been completed from Holberg to Fisherman's Bay, and thence down the east coast as far as Nahwitti, before the outbreak of World War I, landowners may have had some incentive to return to their homes after 1918. As it was, none did so. Funds laid out to provide a telephone service could have added at least a few miles of road, the feature recognized by the settlers from the beginning as the prime need for survival.

It is of course easy to be wise after the event. The Government of British Columbia, perhaps because of the presence of rugged terrain and innumerable inlets, undoubtedly became orientated toward water transportation. Water travel, by steamer, was more convenient and more economical than land travel by automobile. As early as 1910, by which time steamer cruises were already making Redroofs and Buccaneer Bay, fifty miles up-coast from Vancouver, into popular resorts, fifty-mile automobile tours up the Fraser Valley were rare indeed. Along the lower mainland coast, already referred to here, even though a road reached Sechelt as early as 1911, when it could serve only a very small population inadequately, the ten-mile extension to Halfmoon Bay, where a large logging camp operated, was not built until 1930, nearly twenty years later. Powell River, largest single pulp and paper mill in the world, was not served by car-ferry until 1954.

After World War II, when the Union Steamships Company began to curtail its operations, the dependence that had been placed on water transportation, with stops at each minor port of call, became apparent. During spring rains, after some severe winters, roads inadequately ballasted and gravelled became so soft that even Department of Public Works graders were immobilized.

So long, then, as any kind of water transportation could be found to carry mail and freight to northern Vancouver Island river mouths, sand beaches, and shallow coves, both Federal and Provincial Governments remained satisfied. Scores of up-coast fishing villages and logging camps were so dependent on this one mode of transportation that it came to be looked upon as natural and adequate.

But, whereas most other communities existed because of industries located on or near the shore, north end settlers, miles from the nearest landing, could hardly be served by water transportation alone. In later years, as highway and air travel gradually overwhelmed sea travel, these other communities began to suffer. Blunden Harbor, even though lands were surveyed and pre-empted, and homes built, failed without ever having become a community. Bella Coola is looking to road contact more and more for survival. Quatsino, with no road, is not doing well as a settlement. At Port Neville, one of the very oldest general stores, the last vestige of an attempt at settlement, has closed. Shoal Bay, hub of a once prosperous mining-logging-fishing hinterland, is gone now. Refuge Cove, the only traditional supply centre in Toba Inlet, has gone down for a count more than once, and may soon lose its fight for existence. Echo Bay and Simoom Sound are in grave danger. Their loss would leave the entire mainland shore from Minstrel Island to Rivers Inlet without a permanent supply outlet. Alert Bay and Sointula would undoubtedly diminish in significance if the car-ferry that brings a road-end to their communities were to cease its operation. Ports of call which the venerable *Tees* and *Queen City,* and their replacement, the *Maquinna,* could keep busy for over half a century have suffered from the air age.

I was due to be born in August of 1917. Had I been expected at any other time of year, my mother would have had to make a special trip to Alert Bay to reach the nearest hospital. As it was, my birth coincided with the sockeye season. Since most Bella Bella families made their way south each summer to Rivers Inlet to take part in the fishing and canning industries there, Dr. George Darby also journeyed to Rivers Inlet. There, in a small hospital located above Schooner Pass, in Brunswick Bay, he took care of the medical needs of several thousand fishermen and cannery workers brought together at the Goose Bay, Good Hope, Rivers Inlet, McTavish, Brunswick Bay, Beaver, Provincial and Wadham's Canneries.

My mother therefore accompanied my father on this annual trip to the fishing grounds, a journey he had made every summer since his arrival in the San Josef Valley in 1911. Captain Henry Petersen, as he had done year after year, transported the Cape Scott gang across the Sound to the Inlet. Once there, each man obtained a license from the resident Department of Fisheries Officer, and was outfitted with skiff, net and provisions at one of the canneries. My father had fished for the J. H. Todd & Sons Beaver Cannery up to this time. When the Provincial Cannery was built, just after I was born, he transferred to it, midway along Schooner Pass.

Just as he set out on this particular voyage, Captain Petersen's daughter, Johanna Bjerrgaard, one of my mother's closest friends, died soon after having given birth to her first child. When the fishing season ended, my parents had to remain at Rivers Inlet for a few extra weeks, as I had not yet been born. My father and his partner, George Hilroy, decided to buy a pair of skiffs that the cannery was retiring. George volunteered to look after the vessels, taken in tow behind Captain Petersen's *Cape Scott II*. Somewhere off the west coast, the boats bumped together, and George, who was riding in one of them, was knocked overboard and drowned. So my mother and father each lost a very close friend that summer.

During the next two years, my parents divided their time between my mother's pre-emption at San Josef Bay and my father's near Lake William. Now they had to carry not only extra provisions for an infant child, but the infant child as well.

By the time my nearest brother, Walter, was expected, in the spring of 1919, the hospital at Port Alice was in operation. My parents decided to remove to Holberg for this event. There, between stints at earning money for life's necessities, my father joined the Spooner brothers, Dave, Ned, and Jim, at prospecting, a labor of love to all four of them. They were not long in locating a fault that had determined the course of the last few miles of the Goodspeed River. Drilling by hand, they drove a tunnel some two hundred feet into native rock. There, they struck a significant vein of copper and iron sulfide, known to the mining world as bornite. By this time, however, the search for metals had revealed vast deposits of more easily mined mineral than this. Although the potential was there, the experience yielded to my father merely two years of incredible toil, with nothing tangible to show for his efforts in the end.

The Cape Scott-Hansen Lagoon area was by this time almost completely depopulated. N. P. Jensen and his son-in-law, Theo Fredericksen, were continuing to survive by fishing and dairying; and the Wadeys continued to grow produce. George Lovell, whose pre-emption enclosed a large natural meadow, had died, and his widow had returned south.

My father decided that he would make an effort to obtain the Lovell property and take to farming. He found lodgings at the western end of the dyke, in a cabin abandoned by the Holm family.

Our nearest neighbors were the Kris Hansens. The Hansen and Fredericksen children kept the Cape Scott School open well into the 1920's. The Vicks were still at Fisherman's Bay, and Jim Dykes and his family close beside them. Alfred Spencer and his partner, Jim Hooper, shared the dyked meadowlands with N. P. Jensen and the Fredericksens. Harry Widmier, married about this time to Violet Wadey, was struggling to earn a livelihood and at the same time build a new home just below the sand neck. In 1920, we were fewer in number than the Danish colony of 1897, during the first year of its existence.

My first recollection involves a commotion about the dyke sluice-gates, right in front of our temporary home. A storm had apparently carried away a piece of the dyke at that spot. I can vaguely recall men toiling with wheelbarrows to repair the break. Looking back now, many years later, the comparison comes to mind of sailors working feverishly to paint a deck, while fully aware of the fact that the ship was sinking.

My father continued to travel to Rivers Inlet for the sockeye fishing. My mother raised chickens, milked cows, and, as often as she could do so, made her way, encumbered by an infant and a small child, to work her garden planted in a corner of Lovell's meadow. While we could use the property, legalities involved in George Lovell's will prevented our buying it.

On this pre-emption, atop a slight hill, was located a spring whose water remained clear and cold during the hottest summer weather. Each time she made the trip there, my mother would carry a con-tainer of this sweet water away with her. At the dyke, a shallow well yielded a very poor quality of surface water.

Undoubtedly, the poor surface water we were obliged to use at the dyke contributed to my mother's illness during the summer of 1921. After the sockeye season that year, we left the north end settlement, through Fisherman's Bay, the first port of entry.

After having attempted to survive in four different homes through-out the settlement area, my parents were forced to admit defeat. My father had spent ten years on northern Vancouver Island; my mother, almost as long. On each move through the scattered communities of

92

this area, they had left behind not only a house, but also its stove, its furniture, and everything else that could not be carried with them on their backs. Neither furnishings nor home nor land, where all was being abandoned in a mass exodus, could be disposed of for much-needed travel expenses.

Had the depopulation left any one of the minor centres of Cape Scott, Sea Otter Cove, San Josef Bay, or Holberg intact, there might still have been a re-grouping of the survivors into one village. But the abandonment affected the entire north end. Except for the Shuttleworths, who remained at Stranby, the east coast settlements above Shushartie disappeared entirely. Homes that encircled Hansen Lagoon, once the most densely populated community, stood deserted by the early 1920's. The Macjack settlement lost its entire population. Sea Otter Cove, San Josef Bay and Fisherman's Bay survived for the time only because they were mail stops.

Most of the few settlers who hung on could do so only by staying in the homes they had established. Some depended on registered traplines for a livelihood. Some pulled fish-boats ashore on the banks of the San Josef. Some depended on their cattle herds, and thus on the dyked meadowlands for pasture and hay. Some clung to their shrunken store and Post Office duties. The tiny remnant population was thus strung out from Holberg to Cape Scott, some thirty miles.

During the War years, a Development League had been formed, and its members had met to discuss progressive community planning. This movement died with the dispersal of population, but a local branch of the Farmers' Institute continued the fight for improvements to the north end settlements. The efforts of this organization led to an investigation into conditions there in 1922. The *Victoria Daily Times* reported results of this investigation on November 13 of that year:

CAPE SCOTT SETTLERS ISOLATED FROM WORLD MAY BE MOVED SOUTH

To seek a solution of the problem presented by forty isolated settlers around Cape Scott, at the northern end of Vancouver Island, Hon. W. H. Sutherland, Minister of Public Works, went to Alberni during the week-end and conferred with A. W. Neill, MP for Comox-Alberni.

These settlers are without a road. The only communication they have with the outside world is when a boat passes about once a month and even have not got a wharf. The Minister was told that there is a school teacher there who is trying to benefit them a little, *but he teaches them chiefly in Danish. It costs the Dominion Government $300 a head to get mail into them each year.*

The proposal has been made that the Governments move the whole of these settlers down to near some community on Vancouver Island, as this would cost only a fraction of what it would cost to build a road and a wharf for them, as there is nothing at Cape Scott for them to continue.

Dr. Sutherland was accompanied on the trip by Patrick Philip, chief engineer of the department, and Major R. H. Burde, member for Alberni. They examined the road between Nanaimo and Alberni and discussed improvements.

The reply from the Farmers' Institute local appeared in the *Times* of January 27, 1923:

OUR NORTHERN SETTLERS

To the Editor:

With reference to the paragraph which appeared in the daily press of November 13, relative to Dr. Sutherland's plea for moving settlers in the northern part of Vancouver Island to some more suitable locality, it was decided at the recent monthly meeting of the local branch of Farmers' Institute that it was only too apparent that the Minister of Public Works was by no means fully informed or had been wilfully misinformed as to the actual state of affairs obtaining in the district under consideration.

The Holberg, San Josef and Cape Scott districts are more or less interdependent, and form the main settlement north of Quatsino. To remove one is to materially injure the other two. Our interests in the way of roads, schools, transportation facilities and political representation are closely allied if not actually identical. The apparent necessity of such transfer of settlers would surely amount to an admission that the Government was originally at fault in throwing open and reserving this area for settlement, whereas we do not agree that there has been any error in judgment in making this a settlement area. And, be it understood, some eight or ten years ago, nothing appeared to be too good for this then rapidly developing district. Thus no less than $40,000 was allocated as a road appropriation in 1913; a wharf half a mile long was constructed at Holberg to provide proper berthing facilities for the mail steamer in her twice a month trips, and all applications for land at the Government offices were directed to this neighborhood. Houses and small clearings appeared all over the country, to the great encouragement of old-timers. The war, however, with its natural curtailment

94

of local money grants, forced a large number of these newcomers to go out and seek work, and the high wages of the time had rather an ill effect upon their desires to make their homes here. In short, they were landseekers, not home-seekers.

Unfortunately, as a result of this, the genuine pre-emptors, those who had had their full share of lean years before the general settlement took place, now find themselves faced with a further period of endurance. It would be almost impossible to adequately recompense the many who have spent from 10 to 25 years in this area, and it is no exaggeration to say that 75 per cent of the present-day settlers are included in that category. The family man of fifty years of age is no optimist when it comes to making a fresh start in home-building, nor is the young man who for years has given up his trade or calling with a view to making a farm out of the woods likely to be easily persuaded to up-sticks and start over again. Financial compensation of an adequate kind would, we imagine, be almost prohibitive from the point of view of cost, unless it were possibly arranged on some annual payment scheme; but then, what of the hundreds of other small communities, equally or even more isolated and, possibly, a source of just as much expense to the Government in the way of mail service as we are? Although, as the latter is rather a Dominion charge than a Provincial one, it can scarcely be of interest to Dr. Sutherland's Department.

The contention as to the great cost of that part of the road still to be finished is exaggerated, for Dr. Sutherland can not but be aware of the fact that more than two-thirds of the road is already completed, and that the remaining six miles — the connecting link between Cape Scott and Holberg — has been surveyed through and is now represented by a four-foot trail. It is the same road that has been promised yearly for some fifteen years, and it is the non-fulfilment of these promises that has had such a disheartening effect upon the settlers. Furthermore, most of the already small appropriations is of necessity expended on the upkeep of the existing road, and not for the construction of new road. It is a fact, too, that if this road were through, the mail service would be greatly improved and the cost of service largely reduced to all points; and we understand that the Postal Department at Ottawa has already intimated this fact to the Government.

This particular area has proved itself highly productive of garden produce and small fruits; the climate is suitable; the rainfall plentiful; and the valley contains a very high proportion of fertile land. We have at our very doors in Quatsino a market capable of consuming all we can produce for years, and the lucky settlers who can get their produce to this market, owing to their particular location, have always disposed of it with ease.

There can, therefore, be no necessity for removing settlers out — the requirement is to move more in. Spend the money that would be uselessly spent on the negative blessing of compensation upon the positive advantage of a good road — a road, mark you; not a series of weak bridges linked together by mudholes; encourage the settlers by some sort of steamer service, even if a small subsidy has to be paid to the company concerned. Don't discourage would-be settlers by telling them that the land is all taken up, when more than half of it has reverted to the Government on account of unpaid taxes, failure to conform with pre-emption duties, and so forth. And here it should be said that the most unpleasant feature in connection with this is that the reverted land has been sequestrated by the Government under the plea that it contains too much timber to be called Agricultural Land within the meaning of the Act. Having declared this land as reserved for pre-emption, and made the fact public by means of published maps and literature for years, it is scarcely a just act to withdraw the land now, thereby making the individual settler permanently isolated from his neighbors through the interspersion of timber limits in the pre-emption areas. This is not conducive to the peace and comfort of mind of the average settler, and its emphatic disadvantages from the point of view of roads, etc., are obvious.

Given means of transportation, this country will look after itself very largely. Add to its population and it will become a distinct asset. To waste the money that has already been expended upon its development by the proposed removal of the settlers, when the spending of a tithe of that sum would give it the road it so sadly needs, would indeed be madness and would do no harm to the individual, the community and the Province.

We feel sure that Dr. Sutherland would be well advised to go into the matter of this pre-emption area as a whole and not in part, and we are of the opinion that an honest examination of this district by an unbiased and disinterested representative would convince the Minister of Public Works that we do not need philanthropical sympathy, but that we are in very real need of a good road.

In conclusion, when we consider that the various Governments have spent some $200,000 or so (to which the settlers have added their quota in both time and money) in their endeavors to convert this into a farming area, surely it is poor policy to think of wasting *the efforts of both in an attempt to save the comparatively small additional sum necessary to complete the road, which is absolutely vital to the welfare of the country, as well as being a decided factor in attracting the prospective settler.*

Eugene Falck
Secretary and Treasurer.

Eugene Falck's letter exhibited a remarkable degree of restraint. If Dr. Sutherland and A. W. Neill were at all serious about the situation at Cape Scott, the only one of the remaining settlements they apparently proposed to evacuate, they should obviously have travelled to Cape Scott. To discuss the matter somewhere between Nanaimo and Alberni merely served as a pretence of an investigation of the northern end of the island, from a point of view which was meant to seem to be far north to credulous readers.

The comment that a passing steamer called once a month shows that neither the Minister of Public Works nor the Member of Parliament remained in touch with this isolated district. No steamer had stopped at Fisherman's Bay since 1907. A steamer had obviously never called at San Josef Bay, where the boat landing was located more than a mile up the river. It was loss of steamer service that destroyed the Cape Scott colony settlement.

As to a teacher teaching "chiefly in Danish", "Professor" Karl Christiansen had left Cape Scott in 1909, when the original colony had dispersed. Succeeding teachers were of British origin and, since almost all of the original Danish settlers had left the Cape, most students, during peak population years, also came from homes of British ancestry. Neither the British nor the Danish parents appreciated the Cockney accent their children were acquiring about the year 1922.

With two avenues of action open, the Federal and Provincial Governments chose neither. What was done was nothing. The Cape Scott settlers were not moved. The six miles of road to connect ends up-island from Holberg and down-island from Fisherman's Bay were not built.

In 1924, the Widmiers gave up the struggle, just after having moved into their new home at the sand neck. They spent the winter with our family at Gibson's Landing, at the entrance to Howe Sound, where my parents had settled the year before.

Throughout the months we were together, conversations turned, again and again, to the years spent at Vancouver Island's north end. Bits and pieces of information, told from nostalgic points of view,

97

gradually accumulated in my imaginative memory. There, they put together a world even more real than that which I saw around me; for each image remained fixed and unchanging. Since each image arose out of some particular story or comment, the whole of which I accepted unquestioningly, I thenceforth inevitably associated the one with the other, giving to the whole pieced-together picture a sort of fictional quality. Since no image and no comment were ever required to face the tests of time, I created a world held in suspended animation, in which all events merged and occurred simultaneously; fixed, clear, and positively true. My mother, especially, continually referred to a day when we would return north.

My mother, and my two brothers, Walter and William, and I did return, in June of 1930. We travelled up the coast from Gibson's Landing aboard my father's small gill-net boat. After a stormy voyage, he left us at Port Hardy, on his way to Rivers Inlet. We travelled by automobile over the route to Coal Harbor which our mother had walked twenty years before.

At Coal Harbor, the Holes, who had spent some years in the wilderness of Nahwitti, had built a home provided with extra rooms for travellers. The next day, Andrew (Anders) Hansen appeared on his regular mail, freight and passenger run. As we were the only passengers on his boat, Andrew and our mother talked of old times throughout the twenty-four-mile trip to Holberg.

From here on, mother was back "home". After a night with the Hansens, Andrew offered to take us in his Model "T" Ford to the road end, eight miles toward Cape Scott. This was the only automobile north of Coal Harbor.

About three miles out of Holberg, we passed the home of Ned Spooner, one of my father's former partners in the bornite claim. Mrs. Spooner had married Ned after the death by accident of her first husband, A. C. Andersen. From her first marriage, she had two daughters, Francis and Jenny.

Not far from the old Goodspeed bridge, which my grandfather had helped to build in 1910, we saw the Kris Hansen family home. We had lived in this same house when I was about three years old — our second home in Holberg — and when we had moved from here to the Hansen Lagoon in 1920, the Hansens had been our nearest neighbors there. Kris had managed to survive in the settlement he had helped form many years before. He and his wife were to remain there for many years to come, moving out only after their sons and daughters had one by one grown and left home.

A mile or so beyond the bridge, we passed near Swan Lake, beside which Sam Jensen, one of the original Cape Scott colonists, had built his home when the colony had disbanded. Another half-mile or so brought us to Sharp Creek, the first main tributary to the San Josef River on this eastern side. Bernard Dane, who undertook to recount some of the north end story after the settlements from Holberg north no longer existed, heard and recorded a rather strange story about the naming of this stream. Early in the century, so "Teddy" Dane learned the relation from George Ildstad, whose family had formed a part of the Quatsino Norwegian settlement, a man who called himself John Sharp had arrived in Quatsino Sound, and had settled in a cabin at Coal Harbor. He acted as watchman at the old coal mine property there part time, and trapped mink and marten. One of his traplines apparently reached the creek which was later to bear his name.

Although George was only a young boy, the old man befriended him. When under the influence of drink, he would tell the boy many stories of the Civil War, and said that his real name was not Sharp, but that he was actually William Clark Quantrill, the guerrilla raider who had pillaged Union towns in Kansas and Missouri. In 1907, he was recognized by a man who had fought against the Quantrill gang in Kentucky. The story broke in the Victoria *Colonist*. Several weeks later, two men, unmistakably Southerners, arrived in Victoria and took passage on the steamer *Tees*. On the trip up the West Coast, they apparently made enquiries about "an old man named Sharp". The two men left the *Tees* at Quatsino and arranged transportation to Coal Harbor. They returned in time to board the *Tees* for the return trip, and were never heard of again.

At about the time the steamer was leaving Quatsino, George Ildstad called at his old friend's cabin at Coal Harbor. He found Sharp — or Quantrill — lying in his bunk, conscious but with his face and hair covered with blood. George ran for help. The men who went to his assistance asked the beaten man to identify his attackers, but he would only ask for whiskey, and he died a few hours later without having revealed anything of the mystery.

It was said that chest and shoulder scars on the body coincided closely with wounds Quantrill was known to have suffered.

Later, George Ildstad told what he knew to Bruce McKelvie, Victoria newspaperman and historian.

Whether or not the unfortunate soul whose life ended in violence at Coal Harbour in 1907 was the notorious outlaw from far-away Civil War Missouri can never really be known. In any case, the identity of John Sharp, apart from the fact that he left his name to a stream there, forms no significant part of the north end story. Many who made their way to this remote tip of land almost surrounded by the Pacific Ocean left old identities — and sometimes even names — behind them, sealing shut doors to their pasts that never opened again. Since nothing of their pasts became known, only their stories from their new land can be told. If the wanderer who arrived at Coal Harbor in 1900 had been William Clark Quantrill, the guerrilla raider, thirty-five years before, he was John Sharp, trapper and mine caretaker, during the seven years he was destined to live there.

A short distance beyond Sharp Creek, the Model "T" took us past the cabin of Jim Cordy. Cordy had travelled to Holberg three years before, to visit the Spooner brothers, with whom he had worked at mining before the Great War, and had stayed on. Andrew Hansen told us that another newcomer, Earle Lincoln, had recently taken over an abandoned pre-emption in the "South Country".

We stopped at the home of Knute Hansen, Andrew's brother, for lunch and a visit. Knute and Andrew had each built three homes since the two brothers had joined the colony at Cape Scott more than thirty years before. Knute's wife had come out from England to marry him. She took great pride in her San Josef Valley home, and never lost her appreciation of her adopted community.

Here, at Knute Hansen's, the road ended. The trail beyond this point had been cleared to a width of four feet, and culverts and bridges suitable for road use were in place; but it was still only a trail. A very long half mile along a route my mother had hiked again and again brought us, loaded with our packs, to the home of Bernt Ronning, and, across the trail, Willie Hecht's cabin. Both men had just left for Rivers Inlet.

Just beyond Ronning's home, which stood surrounded by plants, shrubs and flowers from all around the world, we stopped to rest at Alfred Lovik's. When a boy in Norway, Alfred had lost all but a part of every finger on his left hand while attempting to pick the charge out of a blasting cap. The loss hardly seemed to handicap this powerful man. He could use a gun, wield an axe, build a home, and even milk a cow with fascinating dexterity. During World War I, Alfred had made enough money from trapping and hand-logging in Kingcome Inlet to live in retirement through the years to come.

Henry Ohlsen met us here and, when we were ready to go, took some of our burdens. At sixty-two, he could still carry a loaded packboard mile after mile over north end trails. Following his brisk pace, we completed the last five miles of our journey, for a two-month holiday visit at San Josef Bay.

As Cecil Ashby, A. P. Anderson, and Ben Luding were also away at the fishing grounds of Rivers Inlet, we missed seeing half of the population of the San Josef area that summer. Apart from my grand-uncle, Henry Ohlsen, all that remained were Jack Rayfield, who now lived in the abandoned Arthur Owen Jones home, a half mile up the river from Ohlsen's, Ashby's daughter Monica and her brother, John, another mile or so up-stream, and Charley Verner and "Old Mac-Donald, at Lake Erie. We saw "Old" MacDonald two or three times during that summer, and found him very keen to converse with others — a most unlikely sort of person to be spending his life as a virtual hermit. Charley Verner, a true recluse, I cannot recall having seen throughout our entire stay.

Monica and John Ashby we saw many times. It was obvious that, while neither complained, they both hungered for human companion-ship. Since the line was located along the Lake Erie trail, far from their home, the Ashbys had not been able to benefit from the Govern-ment telephone system. When she could not leave home to visit, Monica would often send John with messages to my mother. I was privileged to see only a very few of these missives — only some of the poetry. Although I was too young to rate as a mature critic, even I detected in these writings — perhaps because I resounded emotion-ally to poetry — a sensitive and talented soul. Tutored entirely in her own home, as there had never been a school at San Josef Bay, and aided only by correspondence courses, she not only mastered perfect form, but also developed a unique style in her writing. Partly, perhaps, because she had so few persons with whom to converse, Monica had learned to express herself as readily in writing as in speech. She never permitted herself to talk of her imagined world, but, when afforded the opportunity, she allowed it to come to life in the written word. John, her younger brother, without a playmate of his own age, peopled the woods about his home with imaginative friendly neighbors.

Much of the country we had returned to see we visited in the com-pany of Monica and John Ashby. We hiked to Lake Erie; through A. P. Andersen's meadow to visit with Alfred Lovik; and to my father's cabin on Section 26, south of Lake William. We made many excursions to the sand beaches. On such occasions, Monica and John would usually come down the river in their dinghy. Leaving it moored at the landing, we would all board the Government skiff still kept there, and drift down the river with the morning ebb tide.

Somehow it did not seem strange to us that we should have so much beach all to ourselves. The sand, packed hard enough to sup-port a racing car, seemed to stretch without limit in both length and width. Myriads of tiny shells, with large sand dollars dominating, lay in unending patterns where tidal currents had shifted them up the gradually shelving bottom from deep water far out in the bay.

We walked along this white sand the two miles to our mother's cabin, where I had spent the first months of my life. En route, we passed by a peculiar rock formation protruding from the beach, like a huge hand, and known to our mother as "The Mitten". We saw part of a great coil of rope that marked the site of the buried hulk of some sailing ship wrecked back in the nineteenth century. Nearby, we examined the cave, and explored beautiful little Hungry Island, accessible on foot during low tide, facing it. We saw the huge mussels and barnacles my parents had cooked and found quite tasty, and we looked for the tiny pink seed pearls they had discovered in some of the mussels that grew near the sand.

Our mother showed us where our father had watched with fascination as a great ring of crows, all facing inwards, had tried an offender, who paced the sands, awaiting the decision of his peers.

My brothers and I found a baby deer lying in a hollow atop a huge pile of sea-grass. I folded its long legs and carried it, completely passive in my arms, to our mother. "See!" I exclaimed. "It is so young that it can't walk yet!" Holding the little creature under the body, I let its legs unfold. As soon as its feet touched the sand, it shot off like an arrow for the tiny wooded island. Search as we might, we could not find the fawn again.

Once, Monica and John brought down the river a cannery skiff that their father had acquired from Rivers Inlet, upon his retirement from the fishing fleet. This time we did not stop at the river mouth, but, on a tide just beginning to ebb, we continued on into San Josef Bay. It was a clear, warm day, and the sea was calm. At a leisurely pace, rowing in relays, we progressed along a rather informal course from island to island that dotted the pocket known as Little South Bay. On one of these — just a tiny islet — we found a skeleton compressed into a beautifully formed square cedar box. Monica theorized that these remains were of a personage of note, and that she — as the tapered skull indicated — had been given exclusive use of this final resting place.

On another occasion, we located the trail to Section 26, and followed it up to our father's abandoned cabin. The roof was still intact. Not a pane of glass had broken. Here was where I had spent a part of my life too far back for memory to reach. All of the pathetically few items of utensils and furniture remained, so our mother said, just as she and our father had left them, when they had closed the door for the last time. Outside, we explored the natural hilltop meadow that our father had ditched and fenced in order to "prove up" on his pre-emption. In spite of the companionship of one another, we all seemed to feel lonely here.

Later in the summer, my mother and I set out to visit the Fredericksen family, at Cape Scott. The entire journey was new to me, but my mother could recall the identity of each deserted place as if she had passed that way only the day before. Not until we reached the meadows of Hansen Lagoon did we encounter humanity. There, Alfred Spencer was making hay. After a short visit — and lunch — we set out for the dyke.

There, for the first time, flashes of recognition came to me. The dyke itself. The pool above the floodgates, with a half-round cedar log, still floating, on which I had once played. The house in which we had spent our last days on Vancouver Island.

Then, the road through the woods. Recollections ceased again, as we travelled beyond the ken of my childhood. At Deep Bay, the wagon-road followed the beach for much of the remaining way to the sand neck.

Here, the Fredericksen family lived on a site steeped in mythology and history. Their home stood on the northern edge of the sand portage across which native Indians had once skidded their dug-out canoes in stormy weather, to avoid rounding the cape. On their beach to the Queen Charlotte Sound side lay the flat green boulder indented with the footprint of Kane. On the Pacific Ocean side stood the midden remains of bygone Nahwitti occupancy. Something more than a mile from their house, the farthest corner of their pre-emption and the uttermost tip of Vancouver Island coincided at Cape Scott itself.

Throughout the reaches of time, an observer on this 150-foot eminence could have watched the now nameless flow of craft which passed the island's outer tip. The shell midden a mile from the Cape may well have been left there by Nahwitti sentries posted to look for and to signal the approach of any suspicious vessel.

In 1910, the Department of Transport had established a manned light on Triangle Island, the most westerly of the Scott Islands. The light, 700 feet above sea level, was of the first order, with powerful lenses giving a calculated range of visibility of thirty-five miles from all approaches by water. In 1919, because heavy clouds obscured this light most of the time, it was abandoned. In 1927, an unwatched automatic occulting white acetylene gas light was established on the Fredericksen property, at Cape Scott. A manned light is now located at this spot.

I found the Fredericksen locale a fascinating place to explore. Everywhere were remnants of the past labors of N. P. Jensen, Mrs. Fredericksen's father, to reclaim the sand neck for hay meadow. Much of his erosion palisade remained, but the Queen Charlotte Sound side of what had once been a large, productive field was being inexorably returned to sand. Unaware of the disappointed hopes involved in this reversion, I passed my time building tunnels and roads through and around grass-capped dunes, hour after hour.

Lars, the eldest son, was away at Rivers Inlet at the time of our visit, but Hans, a few years my elder, Anna and Ellen, about my own age, and Freda, a few years younger, were at home. Together, we hiked about the sand neck area. The beaches were especially interesting. Beautiful white belts of sand stretched for miles along either coast. Here, all manner of exotic things appeared, as if by magic. Just before our arrival, a new Haida canoe had drifted into Erasmus Hansen Bay. During the previous winter, the family had harvested fresh oranges, day after day, as each tide renewed the supply from some unknown source. Always, especially after storms, Japanese glass fishing floats of varying sizes made their way ashore. Hans gave me one partially filled with water, and one almost entirely filled. Until they were lost in a fire some ten years later, I could detect no loss of liquid from either of these beachcombed items.

These floats ranged in size from a grapefruit to the largest pumpkin. Most were of greenish glass, but a few were of Royal purple. Samples of these beautiful glass objects, gathered over a period of many years, lined paths and garden patches about the home. In the boathouse, hundreds more, for which no immediate use could be found, lay heaped in spare barrels.

The Fredericksen family, at a time when all around them they could see only the deserted homes of their once-busy community, maintained the calibre of enthusiasm and morale of adventurers setting out on their first expedition. When the Cape Scott School closed, Clara, the eldest, turned teacher, and supervised all of the younger brothers and sisters at their correspondence course studies. From Monday to Friday, school was in session in the living room during prescribed hours. When my mother and I were there, Hans was enrolled in grade ten, and was experiencing difficulties with his French pronunciation and with his mathematics course. The day after our arrival, the Reverend William Govier, Anglican missionary, appeared on one of his regular visits. After the evening chores were done, Mr. Govier looked at Hans' papers and coached him, some of the work being beyond the level at which Clara could help him. The good missionary also gave a lesson on the organ, an instrument that Hans played in a style of his own.

In addition to their formal schooling, the Fredericksens also studied, at close range, the natural lore offered them by both land and sea. They could identify every flower; every plant; every sea-shell; every creature that walked or swam; every bird and insect of the air. Widely read, they could converse with an ease that seemed to deny their physical isolation from the rest of the world.

Hanging precariously by a thread, this family lived as if their foundations had remained intact. Knowing danger intimately, they must have foreseen the possibility of the tragedy that was to befall them; but they lived each day with a completeness that excluded discussion of any topic but life.

Later that summer, Axel, younger son of Andrew Hansen, walked up to San Josef Bay for a visit, and, when it came to an end, I accompanied him to Holberg to spend a few days there. Holberg was not really a village then, but rather a few buildings clustered about the boat landing. Most cabins had acted as temporary homes to a succession of inhabitants. Cecil Tenant had by now moved here from the Lake William trail, and two brothers, Chris and Niels Sondrup, had found their way to the tiny community. Chris, when not working or fishing, occupied the cabin we had lived in ten years before, atop a rocky knoll at the wharf-head. A bronze Chinese cannon, lugged ashore from a west-coast shipwreck, and aimed down-inlet, seemed ready to repel invaders from its vantage point beside the old home.

The eastern shoreline of the West Arm at and just below Holberg was lined with enormous steam logging donkeys, all standing idle. To the practised eye, they undoubtedly symbolized the beginning of the economic depression, and the end of the steam donkey engine. To the young, they symbolized the glamorous world of steam. We vaguely imagined ourselves firing one of these huge boilers and somehow or other putting its enormous power to work. Since we could not do so, we made rafts, on which we poled ourselves about the shallow bay.

Six years later, early in May, I travelled to the north end again, entering by way of Shushartie and Fisherman's Bay, the route by which the family had left fifteen years before. Now, walking the trail to San Josef Bay alone, I began to experience for the first time the sense of emptiness and desolation that pervaded the depopulated settlements. The feeling was intensified rather than lessened by the appearance of each abandoned home that stood along the way. Fashioned from prime cedar, buildings still stood intact. Clearings were green with new grass. Daffodils, tulips and lily of the valley bloomed, amid beds of natural bleeding hearts and violets, in their accustomed season. Sometimes the feeling that *someone* must surely be at home became so powerful that the urge to tap on an unlocked door could hardly be restrained.

My grand-uncle, Henry Ohlsen, had written to me, asking if I would look after his place while he spent some time in the Port Alice Hospital. Soon after my arrival, Julius Rasmussen made his monthly visit with mail and supplies.

After the death of Captain Henry Petersen in 1924, Eugene Falck had undertaken the west coast run between Quatsino and Cape Scott with his *Kinky Kid*. Julius Rasmussen had next taken over the run. By 1930, he had sold the *Kinky Kid* to Neils Hansen, and had acquired a new troller-model vessel, the *Promise Well*. It was this craft I watched Julius bring up the San Josef River. My grand-uncle would go out on the *Promise Well,* and return, he hoped, on the scheduled June trip.

Before leaving, he gave me instructions on how I was to behave toward his tiny remnant of Post Office and store customers: what supplies each would want; how each would pay; what assistance I should offer. He took special pains to coach me on the protocol I was to observe when Charley Verner made his appearance. Charley would knock at the door. I would let him in, without greeting him in any way. Charley would sit there. I should sit here. Under no consideration must I utter a sound for a full twenty minutes by the clock. Then I should say, "Hello, Charley." He would say, "Hello"; then I might chat with him. If I were to speak too soon, he would take offence and leave, my grand-uncle told me. The interview came about just as my grand-uncle predicted. After the agonizing twenty minutes of waiting, I simply could not ask the many questions I had planned to ask this pioneer recluse.

Early in June, Julius Rasmussen brought Henry Ohlsen back up the San Josef River. About the middle of the month, Lars Fredericksen came up to the boat landing for me. With Cecil Ashby and his son John on their small vessel, we shot out through the breakers and made our way to Cape Scott. From there, next morning, with Andy Donaldson added to the fleet, we headed across Queen Charlotte Sound to Table Island; and from there, early next day, travelled to the Provincial Cannery in Rivers Inlet. There, and at other canneries, the last of the Cape Scotters were arriving to take part in the same sockeye salmon harvest that had brought the first Cape Scotters to the inlet nearly forty years before.

As a diversion, during the strike which prevailed throughout most of that season, I painted strange names on some of the Provincial gill-netters. Lars' craft, because of its unusual color, I dubbed the *Black Barnacle,* a designation well known at the time as the name of the Sea Hags' barge in the Popeye comic strip. Most boat owners removed the impromptu inscriptions; Lars retained his.

Within six months, I was back into the heart of the north end. My partner, Roland Spencer, and I had obtained a trap line, reverted by Bill Yeo, twenty-five miles around its borders, enclosing Lake Erie, Lake William, and Lake Brink.

Five miles inland from San Josef Bay, on a trail to Lake William long overgrown, we managed to locate the cabin once occupied by Ben Luding, in which to spend the next two months.

The only living being on or near our great expanse of forest, stream and lake was Charley Verner, whom we never saw. Wherever we walked, we came upon deserted buildings. Now, in the middle of winter, they looked deserted indeed.

Roland and I were not typical trappers. We took north with us, among other cultural characteristics, the habit of reading. But we had, and could afford, absolutely no reading of our own, and we had no funds for the luxury of kerosene.

Abandoned cabins, strangely enough, supplied both these needs. We found that most lamps had been left partially filled. The oil was weak, and gave a peculiar bluish light, but it did burn. And most cabins were supplied with copies of *Hunter, Trader, Trapper Magazine,* through 1914 and into 1915. There were no exciting stories, and little about the sort of country we travelled through each day; but we did absorb a fund of useless knowledge concerning the weaponry of a generation before our own.

The year 1915 may have merely marked the expiry date of these subscriptions, but coming upon it again and again gave to it a note of seeming finality probably not too far from the truth.

With Bernt Ronning, Alfred Lovik, and Willie Hecht toward Holberg, Henry Ohlsen and Jack Rayfield at San Josef Bay, and the Fredericksens at Cape Scott, we did manage a fair bit of visiting. During such occasions, we — and perhaps our hosts, too — could suspend our realization that the end was very near.

N. P. Jensen, his daughter, Mrs. Theo Fredericksen, Knute Hansen, Jack Rayfield, and Charley Verner all died within a very short interval of time. In 1938, Lars and Hans Fredericksen went down with the *Black Barnacle.* Alfred Lovik and the Ashbys moved south. In 1941, when the Department of National Defence expropriated their Cape

Scott pre-emption, the remaining Fredericksens moved to Nanoose Bay, farther down the island.

In 1944, Henry Ohlsen died, in the presence of his daughter Violet, and was buried, not in the cemetery plot he had donated for community use, but beside his mother, in an unmarked grave, in his strawberry patch. With his passing, forty years after his arrival, the Post Office at San Josef Bay came to an end. Alfred Spencer persisted at the Lagoon meadowlands until 1956, then gave up and moved to Quatsino. Following major surgery, Bernt Ronning spent his last days in Vancouver. A. P. Andersen, after a desperate struggle with the Provincial Government for a road to his home, left only when he could no longer carry supplies for his survival. At the time of writing, Willie Hecht, who came with the Boytles to Raft Cove in 1913, is the sole remaining pioneer of the days of the bygone settlements. Willie now makes his home at Holberg.

It is most difficult to analyze individuals from past generations, for we can never completely comprehend the sort of world they lived in, or their attitudes toward it.

People who travelled to a corner of the earth as remote as Cape Scott, moreover, constituted no random sample of humanity. Few were so young that they were making their way for the first time; most had tried, and had tired of at least one undertaking in a populated community; and they purposely sought out the comparative isolation offered by a settlement such as this to begin anew.

In a sense, in fact, many sought only isolation; they chose their one hundred and sixty acres of empty land at Victoria, and then set out to find it, two hundred and fifty miles away. The fact that hundreds of individuals pursuing the same inclination formed a rudimentary sort of community was accidental; most of those who chose the Cape Scott area for their new trial would have gone there even if they had known the entire land to have been unpopulated before their arrival. Some made their homes in such remote corners that they saw other human beings only when they travelled out for necessary supplies.

We cannot re-create these people, for we cannot re-create the times in which they lived. Settlements are not founded now; they are literally installed. Today's Kitimat, Gold River, Highland Valley, Mackenzie, and Cassiar represent instant versions of Prince George, or Vernon, or Cranbrook; they never went through the experiences the Cape Scott settlements encountered. While individuals may find themselves, through mischance principally, involved in a remoteness in time and space, true remoteness with respect to entire settlements is literally unknown today; and even the wilderness has lost its sense of distance from civilization.

At a loss as to how to define the pioneer ethos, I turned to Jack McCance, talented member of a talented British Columbia family, and married to Mollie Clarke, whose father, Leslie Clarke, and whose grandfather, Charles Wadey, Sr., both made homes in the hills above the Hansen Lagoon before World War I. Jack, a natural renegade, endowed with the artist's sensitivities, who had himself lived a wilderness life, and who had been so thoroughly schooled by older pioneer woodsmen that he has retained a wilderness mystique throughout his life, wrote typically random jottings, some of which I quote:

The pioneer is one who believes that there is a better way. This is not to be interpreted that his or her lot is above or below average — as a matter of fact, one's position has absolutely no bearing on the matter. The belief, right or wrong, is the spur.

The fact that such a belief is born to a few scattered souls bears this out. To make better that which exists.

Not having been along this way before, they have no means of assessing the outcome; but, yes, even blindly, they are willing to try.

For life can always be better if effort is put forth.

Real pioneers are always kind by nature, with a natural born instinct for understanding. They are not given to vocalizing unless there is a true thought.

Perhaps their faith in their fellow man begins to perish. If this were allowed to continue, their faith in themselves would also perish.

So, in a quiet rebellion, they usually go as near to nature as possible. For in nature there is gigantic peace and grandeur and faith. No one has ever disputed this fact in all the recordings of man. It seems the only phenomenon about which we all agree.

Man is Nature's whipping boy; if only he could learn from this fact. He will never be able to buy his way out.

The pioneer does not question this situation, but goes his way. Not, I believe, to accomplish any specific deed, but to throw off the yoke, if only for a short time.

The yoke — much like, on that rare morning, the good stretch, before the mind considers the tasks for the day. For one brief moment — complete freedom!

One day, in the summer of 1930, my grand-uncle and I stood on the San Josef Bay beach, at the edge of the Pacific Ocean. In the process of our conversation, I asked him why he had never, since his arrival in 1904, left the north end of Vancouver Island; why he felt content to stay in this remote spot, now that almost all the people he had known here had gone.

Henry Ohlsen leaned for a moment on his staff, gazing into the immense open space before him. Then he stooped, picked up a pebble off the beach, and cast it out into the bay.

"There!" he said. "I have just moved all of the salt water on earth!"

In all the years since, I have never been able to think of a rebuttal to that argument.

CHAPTER VI

What could have been the final chapter in the Cape Scott Story has, by a strange quirk of fate, become the penultimate chapter, and may actually herald the start of a resurrection. The strange quirk of fate is one that could not have been envisaged by the early settlers on the Cape, and yet it is one that has many historical precedents — a military presence in the area.

In the early days of World War II, the strategic importance of the northern tip of Vancouver Island was quickly recognized, and the Canadian Military Forces capitalized upon the unique geographic location to provide a point of departure for surveillance of the North-west Pacific area.

The first military presence was established at Coal Harbour where a seaplane base was built and occupied by No. 120 Bomber Recon-naissance Squadron of the Royal Canadian Air Force. This squadron had a long and interesting history and was formed in Regina, Sas-katchewan, November 30, 1936. After a series of moves, including Vancouver and Patricia Bay, it was settled into its wartime operational base at Coal Harbour December 1, 1941, just six short days before the attack on Pearl Harbour.

The establishment of the Squadron at Coal Harbour signalled a disruption of the normal tranquility on Northern Vancouver Island as its land and sea planes scoured the area north and west of the Island for evidence of hostile activities. The few remaining settlers on the Cape gazed up in wonder at the droning machines passing overhead enroute to their operational patrol areas, primarily in search of enemy submarines and ships. Although Coal Harbour was not an ideal location for the squadron, the site was chosen because it was relatively free of fog, ice and haze, and yet did not jeopardize the relatively limited radius of action of the operational aircraft of the day. The squadron was equipped with Deltas, Hudsons, Stranraers, Cansos and Catalina aircraft at various stages during its operational life.

Another defence facility sprang up on the very tip of Cape Scott in the form of a radar station, which was a link in the chain of wartime radar detection finder units located up and down the west coast of British Columbia. Construction was completed and the site became operational July 23, 1942, and the unit designated No. 10 Radar Detachment. The site was under the operational control of No. 1 Group, Western Air Command, but was administered by the RCAF Station at Coal Harbour. It remained operational throughout the war until ultimately disbanded June 19, 1945.

The installation of the radar station at Cape Scott was carried out in utmost secrecy, since radar was still in its infancy and a relatively unknown quantity. The few remaining settlers on the Cape knew the station only by the local name of the "Wireless Station", but were never aware of its true role. The settlers frequently encountered personnel from the radar station on local trails since they obtained many of their supplies from the parent station at Coal Harbour. Transportation from the head of Holberg Inlet was possible by jeep on the old Government Road as far as Ronning, but the final leg of the journey to the Cape was completed on foot, utilizing the same tortuous trail used by the early settlers some fifty years earlier. A communication link was established between Cape Scott and the parent station at Coal Harbour, and this was maintained by a Corporal and fourteen men who regularly inspected and serviced the telephone lines.

With the war approaching its final phases, the operational flying squadron at Coal Harbour was disbanded May 1, 1944. But this was not the end of the facility, since a large whaling station was established, making use of the old hangars and ramps. This whaling operation continued until 1969, when the scarcity of whales made the operation no longer profitable. Many of the old buildings remain, however, still garbed in their dull green camouflage paint, and some are even occupied as private residences.

The radar station on Cape Scott was disbanded June 19, 1945, and all of the buildings, facilities and much equipment abandoned *in situ*. The old barracks still stand today as a stark reminder of the grim war years, but they have been totally cannibalized, and only the shells of what were once comfortable barracks, hospitals and messes remain. All of the plumbing fixtures and items of value were removed by vandals and cached in various locations throughout the north island, presumably with a view to installing them ultimately in cabins at some future date. It is somewhat incongruous today to stumble across gleaming sinks, flush toilets and bathtubs in an apparent wilderness.

After the war there was a brief flurry of activity once again on the Cape when an enterprising entrepreneur sold a vision of fertile land, comfortable homes, Government roads and breakwaters to a number of RCAF veterans. A total of twelve families were lured by this magnetic tale, and arrived on Cape Scott bearing all their worldly possessions, including washing machines and other modern appliances, on the understanding that power would be available. Instead of the Utopia that they expected, all they found were the gaunt and stark remains of the old deserted barrack blocks. Enthusiasm quickly dropped into disillusionment. All twelve families left the area, losing considerable money and abandoning their worldly possessions to the ravages of a hostile climate. All that remain today are the gaunt shells standing in mute testimony to more dreams shattered on the rocky shores of Cape Scott.

Meanwhile, the head of Holberg Inlet was the scene of considerable logging activities. The logging industry had expanded to a point where the largest floating logging camp in the world was established at the head of the inlet. With the expansion of the logging operations, the loggers ultimately established a centre of operations on land, and families came in to create a semi-permanent atmosphere in the wilderness. Under the control of the Alaska Pine and Cellulose Co., a network of logging roads spread from the head of Holberg Inlet to provide the means of garnering the lush stands of timber in the area. This activity enhanced the life of the few remaining hardy settlers who now had a center of social activity and local source of supplies.

In 1950 a most mysterious event took place that had the countryside buzzing with rumours and excitement. A party of twelve men arrived at the head of Holberg Inlet in a boat that appeared to be of government design but yet carried no markings. The men spoke to no one and disappeared into the bush for a period of some two weeks. Local residents observed activities taking place in the bush under floodlights at nights, and strange men moving stealthily throughout the countryside. The group departed just as mysteriously as they arrived, leaving the local residents no wiser than they were before.

The answer was soon to be provided, however, when further parties of workmen arrived and a contract was negotiated with the Alaska Pine Co. to open a road to the foot of Mount Hansen and to the summit of nearby Mount Brandes. Initially, a plank road was constructed, and this was later superseded by a gravel road to transport the men and heavy machinery to the new construction site. It was somewhat paradoxical in an age of electronics, jet aircraft, and rockets that this road was constructed in the first instance by teams of horses from the Alaska Pine Co.

Nestled at the foot of Mount Hansen, a miniature town arose from the forests and mud and debris. In stark contrast to the austerity of the early settlers' homes that still dotted the countryside, modern bungalows appeared in neatly landscaped rows. Meanwhile, on Mount Brandes some five miles away, heavy construction machinery began to level the top of the mountain in preparation for further mysterious construction. All the while a great air of secrecy surrounded the operations, and guards were posted at all the vital entry points to the construction site. Natives were warned not to discuss the activities when leaving the area and a great air of mystery prevailed. One interesting aspect of the construction was the addition of carports to the houses, which was decidedly incongruous since the only access to the site was by boat, and passenger cars were non-existent. These carports were to prove their worth in later years as a means of drying clothes in the never-ending precipitation of the Quatsino Rain Forest.

On the peak of 2200-ft. Mount Brandes, three strange towers appeared, capped by huge white balls, and since these were visible for many miles around both to sea and on land, they added to the air of mystery. The local populace indulged in much conjecture as to the prime reason for their erection.

Ultimately, the reason for the construction became apparent when it was officially announced January 1, 1954 that this was the site of RCAF Station Holberg, which was one of the chain of "Pine Tree" radar stations being constructed across the continent as a defence against the bomber threat to North America.

A few of the early settlers were still in the area, and some found productive labour at the station after many lean years of prospecting, trapping, or brush work. Amongst these were Mr. Ronning, Mr. Cordy and Mr. Lincoln who, although they moved into the station and enjoyed the comforts of warm barracks and regular meals, still maintained their tidy homesteads carved out of the surrounding bush.

The personnel assigned to the station quickly adapted to the sur-

114

roundings and many of the more adventurous, some of whom were directly descended from pioneering stock themselves, started to explore the local countryside and deserted homes of the early settlers. The local place names and those of early settlers soon became household words and the personnel derived a great deal of satisfaction from partaking of the bountiful fishing and hunting in the area. Moreover, they befriended the remaining settlers and to this day maintain a benevolent watch over the old-timers still hardy enough to preserve their independent way of life rather than accept the comforts of a modern home and the pressures of civilization.

Some of the early members of the Holberg Station community became so enthralled by and enamoured with the countryside that they decided to remain, taking up occupations either with the logging industry or with the Station itself in a civilian capacity. Reaction to a posting to Holberg varied drastically from sheer panic to unbridled enthusiasm. One who was enthralled by the environment was moved to put his thoughts into writing. He was one of the early Corps of Commissionaires, who were, and still are, responsible for maintaining security of the Station. A collection of his poems was ultimately put together into a small book entitled "Rhymes of Holberg and Other Works", and became popular with all personnel serving a tour of Holberg. Typical of his work, and a poem that aptly captures the mood of the Holberg area, was entitled "The Song of Holberg Strait":

> The Creator was getting tired
> It was nearing the seventh day.
> "The world I will finish tomorrow,"
> He said, as He hied Him away.
>
> He had finished the rolling prairies
> That border the mighty States,
> He was working along the coastline
> And had started on Holberg Straits.
>
> But the morrow looked dark and dreary
> The mountains looked bleak and bare,
> The rain it came down in torrents
> The valleys looked vast despair.
>
> The Creator gazed long at the inlet
> As He looked from His heaven on high.
> "That place I will leave unfinished,"
> He said with a weary sigh.

115

"Perhaps some day in the future
   The courage to man I will give,
To trim off its rugged edges
   And make it a place to live."

So unfinished it stood for ages
   Lashed by the wind and the gale,
'Til along came a coastal logger
   Blazing a pioneer trail.

A man of knowledge and wisdom
   Understanding, courage and skill,
As he gazed he saw in his vision
   A town by the water, still.

Soon there echoed back from the mountains
   The stroke of hammer and axe,
Soon the shoreline along the inlet
   Was dotted with loggers' shacks.

Trails were blazed through the valleys;
   Logs were hauled through the gap
Alaska Pine had their holdings
   And Holberg was on the map.

Years later, along came the Air Force,
   Making wheels of industry turn.
They built there a site in the valley,
   Near by where the trout streams run.

So, today, should you chance by the inlet,
   A garden of Eden you'll see;
A domestic site in the valley,
   Surrounded by evergreen tree.

The frontier pushed back to the ocean;
   The mountains that hold it in sway,
There's the happy laughter of children
   At home, at school, and at play.

The Creator looks down from His heaven
   As He stands by the pearly gates,
And He smiles at the transformation,
   The outline of Holberg Straits.

John George Wilson

The more adventurous of the station personnel ranged farther and farther afield, and it was not uncommon to find them exploring such remote areas as Raft Cove, the Mack Jack River (the scene of Willy Hecht's trapping activities), the Nahwitti, Shushartie, Brink and William Lakes, Erie Lake, San Josef Bay, Sea Otter Cove and the spectacular bays around the Cape. To provide for creature comforts on these safaris and shelter from the elements, they erected overnight cabins at San Josef Bay, Hansen Lagoon and Crab Island on the Holberg Inlet. By sheer coincidence, the cabin that they erected at San Josef Bay now stands on exactly the same site as that used by Lester Peterson's mother for her cabin more than fifty years earlier. Also by coincidence, the cabin is constructed entirely of logs from the local area and bears a striking resemblance to the original Peterson homestead.

Concurrent with these adventures into the woods came the realization that people would undoubtedly become lost in the dense Quatsino Rain Forest and on the surrounding waters. To meet such eventualities, a Search and Rescue Team was formed on the Station which responds to calls for assistance from anyone lost on the north island. During the past fifteen years, the Search and Rescue Team has been instrumental in saving many lives of people lost or injured while travelling in the countryside.

Coupled with the Ground Search parties, the station supply vessel, the MV *Nimpkish II*, has participated in many rescue missions in the surrounding waters. One of the more significant involved the *Gospel Light*, a small boat used by missionaries to conduct services and to visit the small fishing and Indian communities around the north island. January 2, 1971, the cook stove on the *Gospel Light* exploded and the vessel burned and sank in Holberg Inlet. Fortunately, the cries for help were picked up by radio and the MV *Nimpkish* sped to the rescue. The Rev. Benterud and his family, accompanied by one of the station officers and his wife, were returning to the head of Holberg Inlet from Coal Harbour when the explosion occurred. All seven passengers were removed from the burning vessel and returned to the hospital at Canadian Forces Station Holberg for treatment for extensive burns and exposure before being evacuated to Vancouver by helicopter for further treatment. Unfortunately Mrs. Miller and one of the small Benterud children died as a result of the explosion, but the other five, although extensively burned, were saved. They spent many months in hospital recovering from the injuries. Undoubtedly many of the lives of settlers could have been preserved had such a facility been available to them in the early days.

The old original trail leading from the head of Holberg Inlet to Cape Scott was by this time completely grown over with salal and salmonberry and blocked by enormous deadfalls, some six and eight feet in diameter. Only the more hardy would venture up the trail and endure the hardships to reach the sparkling beaches of Cape Scott. Those strong enough to survive the days of fighting through brush and fording streams brought back tales of miles of virgin beaches lapped by the pounding surf of the Pacific. They also carried home souvenirs in the form of green glass balls that had floated across the ocean from Japan and been deposited high in the sand dunes during storms.

When the B.C. Centennial Committee suggested that each community select a worthwhile project to mark the Centennial year of 1971, it was decided by the personnel of Canadian Forces Station Holberg that it would be a most worthy project to reopen the old historic trail from Holberg to Cape Scott so that the spectacular beauties and history of Cape Scott could be unlocked for foot travellers in this age of jet travel. Accordingly, plans were formed and coordinated with the B.C. Parks Branch to embark on a project of considerable magnitude, a total distance of 18 miles of trail.

Work started on the trail early in 1971, and this soon proved to be no less arduous than predicted. Emulating their predecessors, the volunteers started in with hand saws, axes, and machetes to clear out the old trail and make it passable for travellers on foot. Unlike their predecessors, however, they were also able to resort to the use of power chain saws and brush cutters to assist in their work but, nevertheless, these modern aids had to be carried in on packboards to the work areas and their insatiable thirst for fuel had to be satisfied by streams of human pack horses. The trail was slowly pushed through the tangled debris, following the original trail, up past Lake Erie, and on through the valley to the Fisherman River and, ultimately, to Hansen Lagoon and Cape Scott. The volunteers encountered endless mud, torrential rains and enormous deadfalls that refused to yield even to the relentless buzzing chain saws. Some deadfalls had to be cut by hand with axes and crosscut saws and those that stubbornly resisted movement were indented by footsteps to permit easy hurdling.

Initially, lean-to shelters were erected along the trail as base camps as work progressed along the eighteen miles of trail. These very quickly fell victim to the elements and wild animals, and caches of food disappeared between work sessions. Repairs to power equipment either had to be effected on the trail or the equipment packed out again to the Station.

118

Before starting the trail project, close coordination was effected with the B.C. Parks Branch to ensure that the project was not in conflict with any plans for future park development. The Parks Branch response was instant enthusiasm and through their cooperation, three overnight shelters were constructed by the students of the Shawnigan Lake School. These overnight shelters are now erected along the trail and offer a haven from the elements for the hundreds of hikers who take advantage of the new trail. Formerly, only the most hardy and adventuresome would tackle the hike, but now the journey may be accomplished in relative comfort. Without exception, those who have undertaken the trip have been rewarded by the breathtaking beauty of Cape Scott and the aura of history that prevails in the ruins of the settlers' homes which stand as mute testimony to the courage and fortitude of the early pioneers.

The reconstruction of the old trail has instilled in the Station a great sense of pride of accomplishment, and a greater feeling of belonging in this remote and hostile land. It has reopened areas that were formerly inaccessible to modern-day travellers and the Station receives many letters of commendation from people who, travelling the route, have been enthralled by the spectacular bays, lakes and virgin forest.

Although the ugly scars of the logging industry are evident throughout the Island, it is the fervent wish of those who have journeyed through the area that Cape Scott will eventually become a park and sanctuary for the preservation of the unspoiled raw and savage wilderness beauty that is cape Scott — the land that defeated the courageous efforts of the settlers. Moreover, it is fervently hoped that the day will never come when the long dreamed-of Government Road will come to fruition, since the preservation of foot trails ensures that only those who are truly motivated to follow the paths of the early pioneers can genuinely appreciate the beauties of Nature that make up Cape Scott. It stands as one of the last unspoiled frontiers of civilization, and should remain as a perpetual monument to man's defeat by Nature.

J. D. Dickson*,
Lieutenant-Colonel,
Commanding Officer,
Canadian Forces Station Holberg.

* Now Colonel J. D. Dickson of
Ottawa.

CHAPTER VII

A LETTER FROM MONICA (ASHBY) RASMUSSEN

I am greatly indebted to Mrs. Monica Rasmussen for a letter of recollections appropriate to this book. She grew up on the once hopeful but increasingly isolated bit of habitable land about two miles upriver from the mouth of the San Josef. Let me share this letter with the reader and allow it to speak, eloquently as it does, for itself. No one could have encapsuled more briefly or truly the whole story of the first attempts to settle the Cape Scott region.

I suppose that when one grows up in certain circumstances, one accepts them just as individuals in civilized places enjoy conveniences without a thought of their good fortune. I believe the only things I really missed were the chance of a formal education and the companionship of other young people. As far as home life was concerned, we did not suffer; for, although we did not have much in the way of material things, we were indeed fortunate in having wonderful parents who spoke well, talked of interesting things pertaining to the outside world, and kept up the niceties that made a good home just a little bit better. They also insisted on daily lessons. Mother taught us at first; then, when the British Columbia Department of Education offered its correspondence courses, we were enrolled at once. My file number was 60.

When we arrived in San Josef in 1915, we had a very good general store, owned by Henry Ohlsen. He carried almost everything one could name; but, when lean years prevailed, his stock dwindled to the extent where he could not supply the settlers; and we were obliged to order directly from Vancouver. The failure of his business was through no fault of his own, but rather through his generosity and goodness of heart; for, as money became more and more scarce, he allowed credit to many who were not able to pay. But, if he lost his investment and capital, Henry Ohlsen never lost his greatest asset, that of his staunch faith in God; and that, I am sure, was what carried him through those many weary years.

A Government mail service was provided twice monthly when we first made our home on the San Josef. When the settlers began to move out, the contract was cut to once a month. This was about as frequently as we received our mail, anyway, because for ten months of the year Pacific swells surging into San Josef Bay made entrance into the river impossible. Sometimes, in the winter, we might be without supplies for as long as two months, while the little freight boat laid over in Sea Otter Cove, making futile attempts, day after day, to run the rollers. It was always a big day for the little settlement when "the boat" finally made it; for we, too, had made daily trips, some by rowboat, and others on foot, to the freight wharf, to look for our only contact with the outside world.

Besides garden fruits, we relied a great deal on wild fruits to supplement our diet. Black and red huckleberries, tall bush blueberries, river currants, and salal — all of which grew in abundance — we picked by the bucket and canned.

There were no luxuries or treats, but we were never hungry. There was always a good garden, and salmon were easily caught. These were canned or salted and smoked. I can close my eyes now and smell the cool, damp scent of the smoldering alder wood in the little smokehouse. Meat was scarce, for game had been cleared out by cougars; and there was not enough open land in our area for cattle forage. We seldom saw butter. For a substitute, we rendered lard, added salt and pepper and a bit of onion for flavor.

For Christmas, we usually got a book or a game each; but best of all was our stockings, with peanuts in the toe, a Japanese orange, an apple, and homemade candy. We spent hours prior to Christmas helping to make candy holders from little match boxes — saved especially throughout the year for that purpose — and garlands from the colored pages of Eaton's catalogue, folded into strips, and pasted into links. They looked quite gay hung in loops across the room, and we thought they were wonderful. I remember, too, Mrs. Peterson (mother of the author) showing us how to make tiny pincushions and glue them into half walnut shells, with a bit of ribbon to hang them with; and how to paint faces on blown eggs and tuck them among the branches of the tree to grin merrily down at us.

There was always a community Christmas tree and dance in the Lake Erie hall, and everyone contributed something to make it a success. The bachelors in the settlement cut a huge tree for the centre of the hall. It reached from the floor to the ceiling, and was decked with tinsel and tiny winking candles, which were lighted just as Santa arrived. To us little folk it seemed to go right up to the heavens.

As a youngster, I shadowed Dad everywhere, so it is small wonder that I chose outdoor activities to occupy my time. I spent hours rowing, fishing, and swimming. Later, when I was old enough, I hunted ducks, geese, and deer for meat. At about that time, the deer were becoming plentiful again, after years of almost extinction; but as the deer returned, so came the cougars, close on their heels. They gave us little or no trouble while game was plentiful. However, in time, deer and small game were thinned out by the predators, who became lean and hungry, and attacked several of the remaining settlers.

Ben Luding and his partner, Cecil Tenant, finally left their pre-emptions near Lake William, and built a cabin on the bank of the San Josef River, near our home. They made a circle of rock about three feet high and six feet across, in the centre of the one room. It was filled with stones and sand. On this base they built their fires for heating the cabin and for cooking. In the roof there were two louvers — quite long — through which the smoke was drawn. They said it was the way Indians built their cabins. Certainly it was very cosy, even if a bit on the smoky side.

Radio was just coming in, but money was not, so no radio for most of us. For many years, only two people in the Valley had talking machines. One of these was Henry Ohlsen. His was the cylinder type, with a large horn. That was truly a fascination and, if I had been very good, Mother or Dad could be coaxed to ask him to play it for me. I was well grown up before we owned one, and that came into our possession through the kindness of one of the settlers who was moving out of our community. There were about ten records, and we played and played them until there was more scratch than music. Then, one sad day, the spring broke. Of course, it was impossible to have it repaired; but we loved music, and I can still see my brother patiently turning the discs with his finger.

We were fortunate in having a reed organ. My grandfather had given it to my mother, and it had been shipped all the way from England. When your mother and father were married in the little church on the river bank, the organ was freighted down the river in a skiff, so that Dad might play the wedding march. It wasn't the traditional "Here Comes the Bride", as no one had the music; but I believe Dad gave a very fair rendition of "Clayton's Grand March".

I left the Valley in 1936. I have not been back. Our once cosy home is now a pile of rubble; the faithful old iron range, with its huge warming ovens and copper reservoir, which seemed to hold endless pails of water, carried from the river, lies in a heap of rust. Flower beds, once a profusion of color and scent, are no longer discernible in the covering of salal and salmonberry that has sprung up. Bears have torn out the apple trees, and have left only holes where once our giant strawberry-flavored rhubarb grew. A crop of willowy alders, I am told, now vies for height with the silver maples, poplars, birch, and beech that Dad tended so carefully, long ago.

The wharf, freight shed, and floats have long since gone — torn out by the winters' freshets and gales. The painters have rotted; the last of the small boats once used to cross the San Josef has broken loose and silently drifted, unnoticed and unmissed, down river and out to sea, to be caught and swallowed in the surf, as the others before it. From time to time, many wrecks were exposed on the beach, particularly between the river and your mother's cabin. One week a keel and some planking would be showing, and the next not a trace could be seen. It was as if the sea, despite her cruelty, had relentlessly washed the soft grains of sand comfortingly around the remains of the heroic old ships; and I wonder, as I write, if perhaps, by some miracle, a piece of our own beloved old skiff has been tossed up, and still remains, a mute token of service and of many pleasurable hours.

And shall I ever return? Shall I ever have enough courage to go again to the little Valley that owns so much of me? To see it as it now lies, in abandonment and desolation?

I do not know. Sometimes, the desire to return is almost irrepressible; yet I know it is better that I treasure the Valley as I knew it, with all its beauty, contentment, and happiness, and leave to others the desolation that thirty-five years of time have wrought. For those who rediscover the Valley will know no heartaches as they plow their way through the dense undergrowth along the river; nor will they feel — as I would feel — the sting of salty tears because there are no familiar footprints on the trail or in the sand, nor warmth of home and loved ones at the end of the trek.

But there will be a challenge to those who come — perhaps as hard as, or even harder than, that experienced by the early settlers — those oaken-hearted men and women who expected nothing but hard work, and who asked only for a little niche to call their own.

124

But this challenge will be met in a different way. There will be no rhythmic song of the crosscut saw; no ring of the axe splitting the silent air and echoing from hill to hill. Instead, it will be the buzz of the chain-saw, and the angry snarl of the bulldozer forging through the forest with its fumes overwhelming the fragrant scent of cedar, pine, and balsam that used to fill the Valley.

This will be progress; and, when the Valley again opens its arms to habitation, it will rise above the lost hopes and disappointments of the past. Civilization is now so close to its threshold that there will be no turning back this time; and the Valley, lost for so long, will at last come into its own.

My only wish is that those who follow will appreciate the splendor of the forest, with its soft carpets of shaded mosses, tiny scented star-flowers, and abundance of lilies, the laughing streams, the lazy lakes and the shimmering sands. I hope that they who come may find the peace and contentment that we enjoyed; and that, in doing so, they may find and remember the text scribed deeply into the bark of one tall old hemlock tree: "God is Love, and this is His world."

LIST OF AUTHORITIES

Anglican Provincial Synod of British Columbia. *The Diocesan Gazette,* Vancouver.

Bancroft, Hubert Howe. *History of British Columbia, 1792-1887.* San Francisco, 1887.

Bancroft, J. Austen. *Geology of the Coast and Islands Between the Strait of Georgia and Queen Charlotte Sound, British Columbia.* Geological Survey, Memoir 23, 1913.

Begg, Alexander. *History of British Columbia.* Toronto, 1894.

Bekker, B. Christian. "Wonders Around Cape Scott." The *Daily Colonist.* Victoria, December 20, 1919.

Boas, Franz. "The Social Organization of the Kwakiutls." *Report of National Museum of Canada,* 1895.

British Columbia *Sessional Papers,* 1891-1923.

Broadfoot, Barry. "Trail Blazed to Cape Scott." The *Vancouver Sun.* August 30, 1971.

Dawson, G. M. "The Kwakiool People of Vancouver Island." *Royal Society of Canada,* Vol. 4, 1887.

Dane, Bernard T. Untitled Manuscript on the Cape Scott Settlements.

The Fisherman, Vancouver, May 21, 1971; June 4, 1971.

Government of Canada. *The Official Handbook of Information Relating to the Dominion of Canada, January, 1896.* Ottawa.

Halliday, William May. *Potlatch and Totem.* Toronto, 1935.

Hagelund, William. *Fly the Chase Flag.* Ryerson.

Heyerdahl, Thor. *American Indians of the Pacific.* London, George Allen & Unwin Ltd., 1952.

Howay, F. W., and Scholefield, E. O. S. *British Columbia.* S. J. Clarke Publishing Company, Vancouver, 1914.

MacInnes, Thomas. *Chinook Days.* The Sun Publishing Company, Vancouver.

Nicholson, George. *Vancouver Island's West Coast.* Victoria, Morriss Printing, 1962.

Norcross, Blanche E. "The Lost Farms of Cape Scott." *Family Herald,* March 13, 1958.

——————— "The Sea Always Beat Cape Scott." The *Vancouver Daily Province,* March 11, 1958.

North Island Gazette. Neville Shanks, Editor. March 18, 1971; October 7, 1971.

Peers, G. H. "The Forgotten Country." The *Vancouver Sun Magazine Supplement*. Vancouver, July 5, 1947; July 12, 1947.

Pym, Harold and Irene. *Port Hardy and District*. 1962.

Sharcott, Margaret. "Cape Scott, Land of Settlers' Hopes, Returns to Seagulls." The *Vancouver Daily Province,* July 21, 1955.

Sorensen, Jean. "Beautiful White Sand — And It's Deserted." *Daily Colonist*. Victoria, B.C., May 20, 1973.

Spence, Annie M. "Trader Lyon, First Settler." The *Daily Colonist,* November 5, 1961.

Strange, James. *Journal, 1786*. Madras, 1928.

Vancouver, George. *Voyage of Discovery*. London, 1798.

Victoria Daily Times, November 13, 1922; January 27, 1923.

Wagner, H. R. *Spanish Explorations in the Strait of Juan de Fuca,* 1933.

Walbran, John T. *British Columbia Coast Names 1592-1906*. Government Printing Bureau, Ottawa, 1909.

Walker, John. "Echo From San Josef Bay." The *Vancouver Province*. August 21, 1954.

CORRESPONDENCE

Anders P. Andersen, Vancouver, B.C. (Formerly San Josef Valley)

Mrs. Elsie D. Cox, Quatsino, B.C.

Bernard T. Dane, Victoria, B.C. (Formerly San Josef Bay)

Mrs. Anna Gordon (nee Fredericksen), Bella Coola. (Formerly Cape Scott)

William Hembroff, Courtenay, B.C.

Axel Hansen, Quatsino. (Formerly San Josef Valley; Holberg)

Niels Hansen, Union Bay, B.C. (Formerly San Josef Valley; Holberg)

Mrs. Clara Hersley (nee Fredericksen), Nanoose Bay, B.C. (Formerly Cape Scott)

Willard E. Ireland, Victoria, B.C.

Mrs. Valborg Johansen (nee Jorgensen). Enumclaw, Washington. (Formerly Cape Scott)

Mrs. Esther Jorgensen (nee Thorp), Enumclaw, Washington. (Formerly Cape Scott)

Thomas LaFave, Vancouver. (Formerly Cape Scott)

Michael LeClair, Vancouver, B.C.

John B. McCance, Victoria, B.C.

Major J. S. Matthews, Vancouver, B.C.

Miss Violet E. Ohlsen, Arlington, Virginia. (Formerly San Josef Bay)

Mrs. Dorothy Petersen (nee Rasmussen), Vancouver, B.C. (Formerly Cape Scott)

Mrs. Monica Rasmussen (nee Ashby), Victoria, B.C. (Formerly San Josef Bay)

Alfred Spencer, Holberg, B.C. (Formerly Cape Scott)

Charles J. Wadey, White Rock, B.C. (Formerly Cape Scott)

Mrs. Marjorie Warner, Vancouver, B.C. (Formerly Holberg)

Index

131